The Extraordinary Madness of Banks

Understanding the credit crisis, and the bankers, regulators and politicians involved

Book 5 of The Complete Banker series

By Chris Skinner

The
**Complete
Banker**

First published 2010 by Balatro Limited, 98 Westbury Lane, Buckhursthill, IG9 5PW, UK

ISBN 978-1-907720-10-9

Edited and produced by Searching Finance Ltd, 8 Whitehall Road, London W7 2JE, UK. Tel: +44 (0) 7885 441682; email: enquiries@searchingfinance. co.uk; web: www.searchingfinance.co.uk

Editor: Ann Tierney

Typeset by Deirdré Gyenes

The Extraordinary Madness of Banks

Understanding the credit crisis, and the bankers, regulators and politicians involved

Book 5 of The Complete Banker series

By Chris Skinner

The
**Complete
Banker**

About Chris Skinner

Chris has been providing independent, expert commentary on the key developments in banking for over a decade in his role as Chief Executive of Balatro and Chairman of the Financial Services Club. In particular, he has been writing for various media, such as the Banker Magazine, since 2004 and is a key commentator on banking for prime time news channels including the BBC, Sky and Bloomberg. Prior to creating his independent entities, Chris had key roles at management and board levels covering insurance, retail and investment banking across a range of consulting and technology firms.

Chris has worked worldwide delivering advice, keynote speeches, presentations and workshops to many banks and vendors worldwide, including Accenture, American Express, ANZ, Bank of America, Bank of Baroda, Cisco, Hewlett Packard, Liberty Bank, Lloyds TSB, McKinsey, Merrill Lynch, Microsoft, National Australia Bank, Nationwide Building Society, NCR, TATA, the National Bank of Kuwait, the Union Bank of the Philippines, Wachovia Bank, Washington Mutual, and many others.

About the Financial Services Club

The Financial Services Club is a unique service aimed at senior executives and decision makers from banks, insurance companies, technology firms, consultancies ... in fact, any firm that is interested in understanding and planning for the future operating environment for the financial services markets.

The Financial Services Club bridges the gap between today and tomorrow. It allows you to network with hundreds of professionals all sharing a common interest in the future of the industry. The Club hosts over 50 events a year, in a number of different European countries, with keynote speakers and luminaries from the industry airing their views on the future of financial services. Our illustrious speaker list is targeted to cover all aspects of the industry from practitioners to legislators to futurists.

For more information, go to http://www.fsclub.co.uk

Contents

Chapter 3 Regulators' reaction

Chapter 4 Banks' inaction?

Chapter 5 Too big to fail?

Chapter 6 The bonus issue

Chapter 7 Solutions to the crisis – a personal view

The Extraordinary Madness of Banks

Preface

In this fifth book in the Complete Banker series, I struggled to find a title. After all, what do you call a book about the financial crisis, when there are so many books out there already. *Too Big to Fail, the Storm, 13 Bankers, the Big Short* ... the list goes on. In fact, it's got to the stage that yet another book about the financial crisis would just be boring.

So this is not a book about the crisis. This book is about the outcome.

It tracks the markets from the day that Lehman Brothers collapsed, and before with Northern Rock, through the reactions of policymakers, politicians, regulators and markets. It shows where the weaknesses were in hindsight, and where the pitfalls may be in foresight.

It tries to give the reader a chance to absorb and understand the key movements that created the crisis, and the explanation of why banks, bonuses and bosses are still at the trough feeding and greeding their way through the issues faced.

I use these terms loosely, because one title was going to be *Bulls, Bears, Pigs and Fat Cats*. One of the biggest issues in this crisis has been the reaction of bankers afterwards, with major bonus payments in 2009 and 2010. This has been the biggest issue because, whilst the rest of the world was suffering recession, bankers were still making money and the banks that made these payments were often bailed out by taxpayers. That caused fury and anger, but has still to find a resolution.

Equally, I thought about calling this book *Another Bank Hits the Wall*, but thought it too cryptic. It was a little pun on the Pink Floyd classic track 'The Wall', and the fact that around 500 banks worldwide have hit the wall since this crisis hit would have been appropriate as a title.

Another title was *Crisis? What Crisis?* Another old track – this was the title of a Supertramp album back in 1975 – and again, very appropriate as many would think that after 10 trillion dollars of quantitative easing and bailouts, the financial markets would show some sort of contrition or humility. Nope. Financial markets naturally behave as though there was never an issue, and they do this purposefully because financial markets act like a jungle where only the most adaptable survive.

Anyway, as you can tell, I finally settled upon *The Extraordinary Madness of Bankers*. This is not meant to insult banks and bankers, many of whom are nice people. You may not realise it, but of the millions of people working in banks worldwide, only 0.1% are the bonus boys and girls. That means that 99.9% are just honest-to-goodness branch workers, managers, call centre customer service representatives and similar administrative workers. These folks should not receive the ire and irritation of the public as they had nothing to do with creating the financial crisis.

Equally, you probably shouldn't be annoyed with the 0.1% who make the multimillion dollar bonuses. After all, these folks are rewarded for creating and taking risks with money. That's why they get those bonuses, as the payment is made for generating profits.

Nope, the real irritation should be with the management who allowed the crisis to happen, and that's not just bank management but governance all round. From the policymaking economists to the lack of regulating regulators, the issues are a muddle of many; and their resolution will take years.

So that's what this book is all about, and the title is based upon a classic tale from times of old: *Extraordinary Popular Delusions & the Madness of Crowds,* by Charles Mackay. This is a book written way back in the 19th century, and explains how crowds invest, buy and sell based upon popular mania. It has nothing to do with market forces, but is all based upon market fads. That's what happened here: the market created a fad for wrapping up risk in untested derivatives that proved to be riskier than any before.

This book will show you how it all happened, and is the fifth in our Complete Banker series. If you want to really understand the banking system, then the other books will provide you with a comprehensive knowledge.

Have fun and enjoy the read,

Chris

PS: The articles herein have been selected from white papers, presentations and other research I have undertaken, and from my regular Financial Services Club blog postings at www.thefinanser. com; for more information on the Financial Services Club, go to http://www.fsclub.co.uk

Chapter 1 Anatomy of the crisis

Introduction

The credit crisis origins began in the late 1990s, when JPMorgan's investment team came up with the idea of a new product called the Credit Default Swap (CDS). Within a decade, these products had become all-encompassing in the global financial markets, as they mitigated risk. Many other complex financial products were spawned by CDS, including Collateralised Debt Obligations (CDO) and Mortgage Backed Securities (MBS), along with a large number of other Special Purpose Vehicles (SPV). OK, so I've already introduced a whole range of acronyms that may confuse and bewilder, but that's what happened in this crisis. Investment markets created lots of new bewildering and confusing products that supposedly eradicated risks but instead created the riskiest set of financial instruments ever seen. One of the key things here, however, is that it was all known. Many people saw the risks in these instruments. The failure therefore is that no-one cried out: "it's the Emperor's new clothes". No-one bothered to point out that there was nothing there but a house of risky cards that would eventually fall. Of course, we would shout out today, but it's so much easier in hindsight. So here's the hindsight ...

The credit crisis was NOT a Black Swan event (2010)

One of my holiday books – I'm so geeky dull when it comes to banking – is 'Traders, Guns and Money, Knowns and Unknowns in the Dazzling World of Derivatives', by Satyajit Das. It was recommended to me a while ago, and has been sitting on the bookshelf ever since, like so many books I buy.

This one intrigued me however, as it was written way back in February 2006, 18 months before the August 2007 run on Northern Rock and two-and-a-half years before the September 2008 implosion of Lehman Brothers.

So Nassim Taleb talks about a Black Swan crisis ... this one wasn't. This crisis was thoroughly predictable, as 'Traders, Guns and Money' makes clear.

I dived straight in to the last chapter on Credit Default Swaps (CDS) and Collateralised Debt Obligations (CDO), one of my favourite subjects. There's a good note in there on page 295 about these suckers. Here's a shortened version of that note:

> "CDO logic is perverse. You buy loans and other credit risk from the market, then you cut it and dice it and sell it to investors. It should be impossible to make money. Then why are CDOs so profitable?

> "In the credit trading age, dealers were taking massive 'model risk' to provide investors with higher returns. It was the geeks and their masters who were writing the cheques; they had placed their faith in the credit models; they had started to believe in their lies. Perversely, they were showing massive profits. That's the beauty of mark-to-model. If the model fails, the profit will disappear like a chimera.

> "In 2002 and 2003, benign conditions in the credit market prevailed. Few companies defaulted; people became foolish or brave and lent to companies at ever lower returns; the credit spread on junk bonds reached record lows. Credit standards declined.

> "In 2004, one bank suffered a loss of around $50 million in a single day on its credit dealt books. Nobody really knew why: it was the first tremor."

You get the idea. This book explained all the background to why we would see a subprime explosion and liquidity crisis ... back in February 2006, charting events going back to 2004 and before.

The book cites a court case from 2004 for example, where Barclays Capital were sued by German investment fund, HSH, for 'misrepresentation' after BarCap lost $151 million on one of their CDOs:

> "HSH claims it was mis-sold the products, known as collateralised debt obligations (CDOs), and that Barclays then mismanaged its portfolio of CDOs in a way which further damaged the interests of investors. Barclays also stands accused of 'short-selling' the CDOs for its own commercial benefit."

Barclays argued that the losses were just due to the 'unexpected' downturn in the credit markets, and that HSH was a sophisticated investor and aware of the risks. Doesn't this sound like Goldman Sachs today?

"The risk associated with the securities was known to these investors, who were among the most sophisticated mortgage investors in the world" – Goldman Sachs April 16th press release, in response to the SEC's accusations.

It's a standard defence, as was BarCap's response that it would "vigorously defend" the action as they were "comfortable that these investments were not mis-sold". In 2004, Barclays settled the case with HSH a few weeks before it came to trial as they wanted to avoid the headlines.

A similar case was brought against Barclays and Bank of America at this time by the Italian Banca Popolare di Intra. Again, it was settled out of court.

If you're interested in this stuff, there's a really good presentation on CDO litigation from Jones Day, a law firm, at a London conference in March 2008.

Here's some of the content.

What triggers litigation?
- Unexpected and large potential losses;
- Tripping of over-collateralization or similar tests;
- Disagreement over appropriate priority of payments;

- ◆ Liquidation of portfolio assets;
- ◆ Collateral calls;
- ◆ Poor documentation where ambiguity = opportunity;
- ◆ An unwillingness to compromise or inability to do so due to an encumbered balance sheet.

What are the claims?

America's claims are based upon:

- ◆ Sales practices –
  - ▶ Misrepresentations and omissions;
  - ▶ Collateral contracts/promissory estoppel;
  - ▶ Suitability;
- ◆ Federal securities fraud claims;
- ◆ Mismanagement; Breach of fiduciary duty;
- ◆ Breach of contract –
  - ▶ Contract interpretation;
  - ▶ Third party beneficiary standing;
- ◆ Aiding and abetting breach of fiduciary duty/fraud;
- ◆ Civil conspiracy;
- ◆ Class actions?

UK claims are based upon:

- ◆ Deceit;
- ◆ Misrepresentation (if contract) based upon being innocent/negligent/fraudulent;
- ◆ Breach of contract: contract term/implied term (reasonable skill and care in management of funds);
- ◆ Negligent mis-statement (if no contract);
- ◆ Breach of a duty of good faith/duty to inform.

Who brings the claims?

- ◆ CDO investors –
  - ▶ Senior Note holders vs. Income Note holders;
  - ▶ Institutional vs. individual investors;
  - ▶ Hedge funds/ fund investors;

- ▶ Liquidators and trustees of insolvent CDOs;
- ◆ Swap counterparties;
- ◆ Monoline insurers;
- ◆ Warehouse agents.

Who gets sued?
- ◆ Placement agents\underwriter;
- ◆ Portfolio managers;
- ◆ Financial advisors;
- ◆ Administrative agents;
- ◆ CDO directors and officers;
- ◆ Rating agencies;
- ◆ Mono-line insurers;
- ◆ Accountants;
- ◆ Other professionals? Law firms?

Interesting, and I'll bet this rumbles on for years to come.

Meanwhile, if all this was rumbling along back in 2004 such that a book could be written about it in February 2006, how come no-one – including yours truly – knew what was really happening until the poop hit the fan?

The credit crisis was NOT a Black Swan event (Part Two) (2010)

Could we have forecast the credit crisis? Yes.

Ten years ago in the US, Sandy Weill put great pressure on Bill Clinton's office to repeal the Glass-Steagall Act with some success. This was because Sandy had a vision for Citigroup, which had grown from a retail bank to an integrated bank and insurer thanks to the merger with Travellers.

Sandy now wanted to create a global universal bank, integrating insurance, securities and retail banking, with Citibank, Travellers and Salamon Smith Barney at the forefront.

Trouble was that his plans were being thwarted by regulations, as Glass-Steagall prohibited any one institution from acting as a combination of investment bank, commercial bank and insurance company. This ruling was made after the 1929 Great Depression and stock market crash.

After years of lobbying, Weill was successful, and the Glass-Steagall Act was repealed and Gramm-Leach-Bliley (GLB) came into force. The GLB Act allowed commercial banks, investment banks, securities firms and insurance companies to consolidate, and therefore created the legal platform for Citigroup to emerge.

At the time, we thought the revolutionary model the Act would enable was bancassurance, where more banks would offer full service in-house insurance. Instead, it allowed the riskier activities of the investment markets to infect the rest of the financial operations.

These risky activities would infect the rest of the financial ops regardless – just look at Long Term Capital Management (LTCM) – as the markets are like a house of cards. However, it did create a significant step towards the crash situation we are dealing with today.

Did no-one object? Sure, a few did and, today, the US senator Byron Dorgan is being accredited as the visionary. Here's an extract of what he had to say back in 1999:

> "I spoke earlier today about this legislation, which is called the Financial Services Modernization Act of 1999, and said then that I am probably part of a very small minority in this Chamber, but I feel very strongly that this is exactly the wrong bill at exactly the wrong time. It misses all the lessons of the past and, in my judgment, it creates definitions and moves in directions that will be counterproductive to our financial future.
>
> "What does this bill do? It would permit common ownership of banks, insurance, and securities companies, and, to a

significant degree, commercial firms as well. It will permit bank holding companies, affiliates, and bank subsidiaries to engage in a smorgasbord of expanded financial activities, including insurance and securities underwriting, and merchant banking all under the same roof.

"This bill will also, in my judgment, raise the likelihood of future massive taxpayer bailouts. It will fuel the consolidation and mergers in the banking and financial services industry at the expense of customers, farm businesses, family farmers, and others, and in some instances I think it inappropriately limits the ability of the banking and thrift institution regulators from monitoring activities between such institutions and their insurance or securities affiliates and subsidiaries raising significant safety and soundness consumer protection concerns."

And further proof from the *New York Times* at that time:

Congress passes wide-ranging Bill easing bank laws
By Stephen Labaton, November 5, 1999

"WASHINGTON, Nov. 4— Congress approved landmark legislation today that opens the door for a new era on Wall Street in which commercial banks, securities houses and insurers will find it easier and cheaper to enter one another's businesses.

"The measure, considered by many the most important banking legislation in 66 years, was approved in the Senate by a vote of 90 to 8 and in the House tonight by 362 to 57. The bill will now be sent to the president, who is expected to sign it, aides said. It would become one of the most significant achievements this year by the White House and the Republicans leading the 106th Congress.

" 'Today Congress voted to update the rules that have governed financial services since the Great Depression and replace them with a system for the 21st century,' Treasury Secretary Lawrence H. Summers said. 'This historic legislation will better enable American companies to compete in the new economy.' "

"The decision to repeal the Glass-Steagall Act of 1933 provoked dire warnings from a handful of dissenters that the deregulation of Wall Street would someday wreak havoc on the nation's financial system. The original idea behind Glass-Steagall was that separation between bankers and brokers would reduce the potential conflicts of interest that were thought to have contributed to the speculative stock frenzy before the Depression.

"Today's action followed a rich Congressional debate about the history of finance in America in this century, the causes of the banking crisis of the 1930s, the globalization of banking and the future of the nation's economy.

"Administration officials and many Republicans and Democrats said the measure would save consumers billions of dollars and was necessary to keep up with trends in both domestic and international banking. Some institutions, like Citigroup, already have banking, insurance and securities arms but could have been forced to divest their insurance underwriting under existing law. Many foreign banks already enjoy the ability to enter the securities and insurance industries.

" 'The world changes, and we have to change with it,' said Senator Phil Gramm of Texas, who wrote the law that will bear his name along with the two other main Republican sponsors, Representative Jim Leach of Iowa and Representative

Thomas J. Bliley Jr. of Virginia. 'We have a new century coming, and we have an opportunity to dominate that century the same way we dominated this century. Glass-Steagall, in the midst of the Great Depression, came at a time when the thinking was that the government was the answer. In this era of economic prosperity, we have decided that freedom is the answer.'

"In the House debate, Mr. Leach said, 'This is a historic day. The landscape for delivery of financial services will now surely shift.'

"But consumer groups and civil rights advocates criticized the legislation for being a sop to the nation's biggest financial institutions. They say that it fails to protect the privacy interests of consumers and community lending standards for the disadvantaged and that it will create more problems than it solves.

"The opponents of the measure gloomily predicted that by unshackling banks and enabling them to move more freely into new kinds of financial activities, the new law could lead to an economic crisis down the road when the marketplace is no longer growing briskly.

" 'I think we will look back in 10 years' time and say we should not have done this but we did because we forgot the lessons of the past, and that that which is true in the 1930s is true in 2010,' said Senator Byron L. Dorgan, Democrat of North Dakota. 'I wasn't around during the 1930s or the debate over Glass-Steagall. But I was here in the early 1980s when it was decided to allow the expansion of savings and loans. We have now decided in the name of modernization to forget the lessons of the past, of safety and of soundness.'

"Senator Paul Wellstone, Democrat of Minnesota, said that Congress had 'seemed determined to unlearn the lessons from our past mistakes.'

" 'Scores of banks failed in the Great Depression as a result of unsound banking practices, and their failure only deepened the crisis,' Mr. Wellstone said. 'Glass-Steagall was intended to protect our financial system by insulating commercial banking from other forms of risk. It was one of several stabilizers designed to keep a similar tragedy from recurring. Now Congress is about to repeal that economic stabilizer without putting any comparable safeguard in its place.'

"Supporters of the legislation rejected those arguments. They responded that historians and economists have concluded that the Glass-Steagall Act was not the correct response to the banking crisis because it was the failure of the Federal Reserve in carrying out monetary policy, not speculation in the stock market, that caused the collapse of 11,000 banks. If anything, the supporters said, the new law will give financial companies the ability to diversify and therefore reduce their risks. The new law, they said, will also give regulators new tools to supervise shaky institutions.

" 'The concerns that we will have a meltdown like 1929 are dramatically overblown,' said Senator Bob Kerrey, Democrat of Nebraska.

"Others said the legislation was essential for the future leadership of the American banking system.

" 'If we don't pass this bill, we could find London or Frankfurt or years down the road Shanghai becoming the financial capital of the world,' said Senator Charles E. Schumer, Democrat of New York. 'There are many reasons for this bill, but first and foremost is to ensure that US financial firms remain competitive.'

(...)

"Many experts predict that, even though the legislation has been trailing market trends that have begun to see the cross-ownership of banks, securities firms and insurers, the new law is certain to lead to a wave of large financial mergers.

"The White House has estimated the legislation could save consumers as much as $18 billion a year as new financial conglomerates gain economies of scale and cut costs.

"Other experts have disputed those estimates as overly optimistic, and said that the bulk of any profits seen from the deregulation of financial services would be returned not to customers but to shareholders."

(...)

What do criminals, bankers and Warren Buffett have in common? (2010)

Some years ago, I delivered a presentation as a keynote with the title 'All Bankers are Criminals'. I actually didn't mean 'all'. The chicken feed, battery farmed, commercial, transactional and retail bankers are pin-stripe suited, humble pie, nice guys.

I was talking about the evil animals of Wall Street and the City. These jungle animals hunt you down, rip out your wallet and tear your money apart, note-by-note. OK, I exaggerate a little, but you get the idea.

The theme of the presentation mainly came from Frank Partnoy's excellent book 'Infectious Greed', which traces the growth of 'weapons of financial destruction': derivatives, as named by Warren Buffett in his 2002 shareholder letter.

It is quite clear from this book that unchecked investment markets will run free of scruples and morals. This is what happened with Frank Quattrone of Credit Suisse and the dotcom boom and bust, along with many other examples through history.

It is not necessarily as true when we talk about arbitrage strategies and the John Meriwethers of this world. However, these people are far more dangerous because they create financial markets systemic risk that can bring down companies and countries.

In case you are wondering who John Meriwether is, he was one of the first arbitrage players and built Salomon Brothers into the big swinging dick master of the universe world so brilliantly depicted in Michael Lewis's book 'Liar's Poker'.

With his colleagues, the use of arbitrage instruments led to the downfall of Salomon Brothers – they were subsequently merged into Citigroup – and Meriwether went on to create Long Term Capital Management (LTCM).

In 1998 LTCM lost $4.6 billion in less than four months and became the leading case study for how systemic risk created by derivatives products, combined with massive leverage and arbitrage risk-models, creates a financial deck of cards. A deck that can rise and fall in the blink of an eye, with the latter potentially ruining companies, markets, countries and governments, as happened in the most recent crisis.

Anyways, not to be dissuaded from his cause, Meriwether went on to found JWM Partners, another highly leveraged 'relative value arbitrage' firm. Yet again, he built leverage through this hedge fund from its opening with $250 million under management in 1999 to a massive $3 billion firm by 2007. Of course, it was all just on paper as the latest crisis battered the fund, losing almost half of its value between September 2007 and February 2009. The deck of cards strikes again.

17

It closed in late 2009 and guess what? Meriwether's about to launch yet another hedge fund, based upon just the same concepts.

To me, this is the criminality of the financial system in action. Firms that build highly leveraged derivatives instruments for short-term arbitrage, with unproven skills and massive risk.

Not that I'm calling Meriwether a criminal, as it's all perfectly legitimate under SEC and FSA rules. Or it was. It may be that the Goldman Sachs furore will change all this.

You see, Goldman Sachs, like Meriwether, is very good at taking leverage and risk and managing the markets to gain short-term profit. Like Meriwether, Goldman Sachs succeeded in using these tools and instruments to generate massive profits. They achieved a record 131 trading days last year, in which the bank made at least $100 million net trading revenue each day.

Unlike Meriwether, Goldman Sachs managed to offload and hedge their risks back to others, such as AIG and IKB, such that when the markets collapsed, their clients, suppliers and partners got burnt, but not them.

Nothing wrong with that, as it's all perfectly legitimate under SEC and FSA rules. Unless the SEC and FSA find Goldman Sachs guilty of fraud. But how can they be guilty of a crime that was not a crime at the time it was committed? There's the rub.

I'm sure the SEC will aim to build a bulletproof case, and their cause is a worthy one: clean up the financial system.

Is it worthy to do this so publicly? Not sure. Is it worthy to name the defendant up front, when the burden of proof has yet to be proven? Not sure.

The Goldman Sachs case is actually more like watching a rape trial in action, where the defendant is a shifty-looking guy who probably seems guilty whether guilty or not. The guilt sits there, and that's what will happen with Goldman Sachs.

Whether guilty or not – and they've hired the best team possible to defend themselves, including 'Master of Disaster' Mark Fabiani – we will always associate Goldman Sachs with something smelly for the foreseeable years to come.

The only thing that really gets me is Warren Buffett. The Sage of Omaha has made his billions through prudent focus upon 'value investing'. That means investing in strong and robust businesses like Coca-Cola, American Express, Gillette and the *Washington Post*.

So when he referred to derivatives as 'weapons of financial destruction' in his shareholder letter of 2002, I respected the man and his integrity of thought. Now, having found Goldman Sachs under attack, he has stepped up to their defence, and I wondered why.

Warren Buffett is an intriguing character, as we all know. The friend of kings and kingmakers, he walks a path separate to most. He knows the dangers of arbitrage, derivatives and leverage, because he had to step into Salomon Brothers in 1991 to clean up Meriwether and his colleagues' mess.

(…)

Switch to 2010. Warren Buffett invested heavily in Goldman Sachs in September 2008 – when Lehman Brothers, Merrill Lynch and Morgan Stanley were all imploding – buying $5 billion of preferred stock at a 10 percent dividend. These investments earn him $950 a minute, or $500 million a year today. No wonder he claims to be in love with that investment.

Trouble is that the alleged fraud at Goldman Sachs has really hit their share price.

Thinking back to the observation on Salomon that if *the firm* is 'credit dependent', as Salomon was to an extreme, it cannot tolerate a negative change in perceptions, Buffett must be seriously worried about Goldman Sachs losing its creditworthiness, especially as it depends on good credit.

Oh yes, and having called derivatives 'weapons of financial destruction', guess what? Berkshire Hathaway, Warren Buffett's investment firm, has a massive portfolio of derivatives investments. From the *Wall Street Journal* last week:

"Democrats took a step toward their goal of overhauling financial regulation, reaching a tentative deal to set restrictions on trading in exotic financial instruments known as derivatives. Among the considerations still in the balance: A big provision being sought by Warren Buffett in recent weeks ... the provision, sought by Berkshire and pushed by Nebraska Senator Ben Nelson in the Senate Agriculture Committee, would largely exempt existing derivatives contracts from the proposed rules. Previously, the legislation could have allowed regulators to require that companies such as Nebraska-based Berkshire put aside large sums to cover potential losses. The change thus would aid Berkshire, which has a $63 billion derivatives portfolio, according to Barclays Capital."

Hmmm ... maybe that greed is infectious, although Morningstar analyst Bill Bergman supports Mr. Buffett's exemption by stating that: "Claiming Berkshire poses a risk to the financial system is a difficult case to make."

Either way, the US movement towards an approval of a Financial Reform Bill to handle the issues of banks that are 'too big to fail' takes it one step nearer to the American system taking a lead role towards a new financial architecture.

Derivatives are next ... and Warren Buffett, like Lloyd Blankfein at Goldman Sachs and all of those current and former bankers and brokers who dealt in toxic derivatives across the world, must be worried.

Who can be trusted after the financial crisis? (2009)

Just found a great paper by the Centre for European Policy Studies (CEPS) titled 'Who can be trusted after the financial crisis?' Using extensive research across the EU, the EC, the ECB and more, they draw four main conclusions.

"First, our analysis of the impact of the financial crisis on confidence in the European institutions shows a severe decrease in citizens' trust in the immediate aftermath of the financial crisis with a slight recovery nine month later. In particular citizens' net trust in the ECB hit an historical low point in the aftermath of the financial crisis with a majority of people distrusting the ECB.

"Second, the trend in confidence in European institutions is diametrically opposed to citizens' confidence in the national government and parliament. When citizens' confidence in the European institutions decreased in the immediate aftermath of the crisis, confidence in the national government actually increased. When the confidence in European institutions recovered nine months later, confidence in the national government decreased. However, not all data support this conclusion. Data from the Edelman Trust Barometer suggest a continuous increase in the confidence in the government.

"Third, our analysis of confidence in business and citizens' confidence in banks and stock markets produces ambiguous results. Whereas citizens' confidence in stock markets and business confidence has recovered in most countries, confidence in banks has deteriorated nine month after the crisis.

"Fourth, confidence levels in free market economies seem to have dropped in a majority of countries nine month after the crisis. Only in the German case could one actually detect an increase in confidence in the free market economy. However, separate data sources show that levels of net confidence in the free market economy in the US remain significantly higher than in the two European economies Germany and France.

"Given that in particular in France and Germany a decrease in net confidence is associated with an increase in citizens' demands for stronger state support and that German and French citizens have the highest level of anti-capitalist sentiments, French and German governments will have to invest more effort in trust enhancing policies.

"Nevertheless, one has to highlight that the financial crisis also had a deep impact on the US economy as citizens' demand for stronger state regulation has risen immensely and has almost reached European levels."

A little cloud in the sky (2009)

It's Monday, start of the week, smile on my face and sun in the sky. I should be looking up, pushing forward, feeling fine and seeing the future as bright. We should all be. But there's a little cloud on the horizon called doubt.

Why is there doubt? Because there is a feeling that we have prescribed the drugs to treat the illness but have not cured the disease.

Governments have pumped $11 trillion into the financial system, whilst banks have a further $1.5 trillion to come, according to the IMF's latest figures.

$1.5 trillion still to write off? And most of that in Europe's banks? According to the IMF, there's $418 billion in further bank losses in the USA, $126 billion in Asia and the bulk of the losses – $934 billion – in Europe, with $344 billion of that lot in the UK alone.

So yes, it's Monday, start of the week, smile on my face and sun in the sky. I am looking up, pushing forward, feeling fine and seeing the future as bright. I just don't like that little cloud.

Mind you, what does the IMF really know, as last year they estimated the crisis to cost around $400 billion when it was just subprime losses and then upped it to $1 trillion after the Lehman collapse.

Pah! Doubt has now been joined by Fear and Uncertainty.

Happy Mondays!

Queen to chair debate about capitalism killing the planet? (2009)

On 22nd July, Fellows of the British Academy Professors Tim Besley, FBA, and Peter Hennessy, FBA, sent a letter to Her Majesty the Queen (heavily edited version follows):

"Madam

When Your Majesty visited the London School of Economics last November, you quite rightly asked: why had nobody noticed that the credit crunch was on its way? The British Academy convened a forum on 17 June 2009 to debate your question.

Many people did foresee the crisis. However, the exact form that it would take and the timing of its onset and ferocity were foreseen by nobody.

For example, the Bank of International Settlements expressed repeated concerns that risks did not seem to be properly reflected in financial markets. Our own Bank of England issued many warnings about this in their biannual Financial Stability Reports.

Risk management was considered an important part of financial markets. One of our major banks, now mainly in public ownership, reputedly had 4,000 risk managers. But the difficulty was seeing the risk to the system as a whole rather than to any specific financial instrument or loan. Risk calculations were most often confined to slices of financial activity, using some of the best mathematical minds in our country and abroad. But they frequently lost sight of the bigger picture.

There were many who warned of the dangers of this. But against those who warned, most were convinced that banks knew what they were doing.

They believed that the financial wizards had found new and clever ways of managing risks. Indeed, some claimed to have so dispersed them through an array of novel financial instruments that they had virtually removed them. It is difficult to recall a greater example of wishful thinking combined with hubris.

And politicians of all types were charmed by the market. People trusted the banks whose boards and senior executives were packed with globally recruited talent and their non-executive directors included those with proven track records in public life. Nobody wanted to believe that their judgement could be faulty or that they were unable competently to scrutinise the risks in the organisations that they managed. A generation of bankers and financiers deceived themselves and those who thought that they were the pace-making engineers of advanced economies.

All this exposed the difficulties of slowing the progression of such developments in the presence of a general 'feel-good' factor.

Among the authorities charged with managing these risks, there were difficulties too. Some say that their job should have been 'to take away the punch bowl when the party was in full swing'. But that assumes that they had the instruments needed to do this. General pressure was for more lax regulation – a light touch. The City of London (and the Financial Services Authority) was praised as a paragon of global financial regulation for this reason.

There was a broad consensus that it was better to deal with the aftermath of bubbles in stock markets and housing markets than to try to head them off in advance.

Inflation remained low and created no warning sign of an economy that was overheating.

So where was the problem?

Everyone seemed to be doing their own job properly on its own merit. And according to standard measures of success, they were often doing it well. The failure was to see how collectively this added up to a series of interconnected imbalances over which no single authority had jurisdiction. This, combined with the psychology of herding and the mantra of financial and policy gurus, lead to a dangerous recipe. Individual risks may rightly have been viewed as small, but the risk to the system as a whole was vast.

So in summary, Your Majesty, the failure to foresee the timing, extent and severity of the crisis and to head it off, while it had many causes, was principally a failure of the collective imagination of many bright people, both in this country and internationally, to understand the risks to the system as a whole."

Very good.

On 14th August 2009, a group of senior figures including Professor Herman Daly of Maryland University, Professor Lord Anthony Giddens and Professor Peter Victor of York University, Canada, sent this letter (heavily edited) to the Queen:

"Your Majesty,

We, the undersigned, noted with interest the letter to Your Majesty of 22nd July 2009 from the British Academy in which they respond to your question about how the current economic meltdown was missed. They talked of a "failure of the collective imagination of many bright people" and a "psychology of denial". The Academy wrote "It is difficult to recall a greater example of wishful thinking combined with hubris."

We are writing to you because we are concerned that the British Academy's letter focuses on one particular aspect of current insecurity, namely financial, failing to address the wider context of more serious macro issues facing mankind. We are also writing to the Academy to invite them to debate these issues with us.

We live in tumultuous times. Many developed world citizens are losing their livelihoods. The effects on the world's poorest will, as ever, be dreadful. However, we are surprised that the Academy has not addressed anything outside the narrow remit their letter covered. Far greater insecurities threaten the world's poorest due to our effects on the natural world.

The letter ignores the physical constraints which are central to this bubble and indeed most bubbles. It speaks of "the bigger picture" and of "individual risks being small" and "the system as a whole being vast", yet, for us has a limited horizon.

Our premise is that our current economic malaise is symptomatic of a far more serious systemic failure to acknowledge what Archbishop Rowan Williams has identified in saying

"It has been said that 'the economy is a wholly-owned sub-sidiary of the environment'. The earth itself is what ultimately controls economic activity because it is the source of the materials upon which economic activity works".

Energy is the lifeblood of any economy. Our exponential debt-based money system is in turn based on exponen-tially increasing energy supplies. It is therefore clear that the supply of that energy deserves our very highest attention. That this attention doesn't appear in the Academy's analysis is deeply worrying.

The letter refers to the "overheating economy" but gives no mention of the effect and cause of the overheating of planet Earth.

The Academy's letter mentions unprecedented global eco-nomic growth – yet it fails to mention the rapidly escalating environmental destruction caused by this insatiable growth. It also mentions the poor of the developing world who have been brought out of poverty to 'prosperity'; but not the far greater numbers condemned to an increasingly inequitable world and the ravages of peak-food and climate change.

The letter talks of a "general feel-good factor", but doesn't address the fact that, in the developed world, general wellbe-ing long ago ceased to be linked with GDP growth.

We envisage a society whose primary goal should be the wellbeing of society itself and of the planetary resources and environment that sustains us all, with economic objectives shaped to support that central goal rather than the other way around."

Our current form of corporate-consumer-capitalism has been shown to be what many of us knew it was: a fundamen-tally flawed system which badly needs updating.

It would appear from the British Academy's letter that they are not aware of the rapidly growing and vibrant debate around these issues. We agree with them about the need for "authorities with the power to act" and for appropriate levels of regulation fit for the task in hand. Their prescription is to consider how they "might develop a new, shared horizon-scanning capability". We will invite the Academy to join with us in a public dialogue about these issues and ask them to consider how this 'new capability' can make its primary horizon the issues we raise in this letter. We will of course report findings of such debate to Your Majesty."

I wonder if the Queen could be the chair in a nice debate entitled 'This House believes that capitalism is killing the planet'?

BBC's Robert Peston presents ... (2009)

Robert Peston, the BBC's lead reporter on the banks throughout this crisis and author of 'Who Runs Britain?' presented a discussion I attended the other night.

Robert's presentation was titled 'The new capitalism: the cost of men behaving badly' and, just to be clear, he presented under Chatham House rules so the summary below is purely my spin on what he said, and not his words.

First, an estimate of the losses to date. $4 trillion. Actually, no, it was $9 trillion. That's $9,000,000,000,000.

If a dollar was equivalent to one second, it would take about 11.57 days to get through a million dollars, 31.7 years to get through a billion and back to the birth of mankind 32,000 years ago to get to a trillion dollars. That's $1 trillion.

$9 trillion. $9 trillion of losses. $4 trillion came from the banking industry. $4 trillion of bailouts, cash injections, support and relief. Then a further $5 trillion of corporate losses in lost output through lack of access to liquidity, loans, working capital and trade finance.

$9 trillion. About 300,000 years of spending a dollar a second. That's 25% of the world's global output.

A quarter of the world's output lost due to this silly crisis created by what? Bad maths.

This is best illustrated by the example of Goldman Sachs' black box event back in August 2007. This is where David Viniar, Goldman Sachs' CFO, said: "We are seeing things that were 25-standard deviation events, several days in a row. There have been some issues in some of the other quantitative spaces, but nothing like what we saw last week."

A '25-standard deviation event' only happens once every 100,000 years or more according to the models built into the systems, but then they occurred several days in a row and the Goldman Sachs fund lost $1.5 billion.

In other words, banks were organised and managed using bad science. Now, was that down to too little regulation – 'light touch' – or just bad regulation? To be truthful, it is an indictment of regulation that didn't work combined with a failure of Alan Greenspan's science.

You see, Greenspan prayed to the lords of securitisation and light touch regulation. He believed markets regulated themselves through competitive forces and securitisation worked because it distributes risks widely across the markets. But there were two errors in Greenspan's thinking that went wrong.

The first was the belief that banks only lent money after checking that a borrower had the ability to pay it back; and the other was the belief that banks would lay off risks to others and spread the risks widely across the markets.

The banks did not do this. In fact, they retained risks because, once this was repackaged and given a AAA rating, it was easier to keep on the banks' books as assets rather than spreading them around outside the markets.

And in all cases, the regulators missed this trick because they were looking for crooks rather than idiots. This was not criminal activity, just incompetence, and the FSA and SEC just thought management of these firms were regulating their staff misbehaviours rather than looking for such malfeasance. This is why we expect too much from regulation as, to be honest, there was more regulation than you could shake a stick at before this crisis, and much of it was on a statutory footing.

So this was a failure of regulators, regulation, management and markets ... but the overall failure was not caused by these factors, but more by a failure of theory.

This is because conventional analysis saw the housing and market bubble as harmless, and the theory was that the housing market wouldn't need to be propped up by the Bank of England. But that theory was wrong due to the fact that there was far too much lending at far too cheap a price, and the theory that liquidity would remain stable and available was wrong.

The result is that we borrowed more than 100% of GDP and personal sector borrowing today is running at around 170% of GDP. That's ridiculous. It has increased by around 70% since 2000, and it was unhealthy back in 2000 as a result of eight years of unparalleled growth in the economy.

So here is the horrible paradox: compliance meant that any banker would tell you that regulation was severe and intrusive. The result is that we bred a culture of compliance where, if the boxes were ticked and all ok, then the deal was ok. This meant that no-one asked whether the deal was sensible or ethical, in a more fundamental sense.

It was this culture of box ticking that resulted in the biggest regulatory failure any of us will ever witness. But it was more than this, because the box ticking issue lay with the false comfort provided by experts.

The credit rating agencies priesthood meant that even the Bank of England paid homage to these priests. They gave the best AAA ratings, which were meant to be for the nicest investments, to the stinkiest investments. The AAA rating was given to stinky products because of lousy data and a confusion between solvency and liquidity.

The primary thing they got wrong was using data for defaults and repayment difficulties from the 1990s. This data was created when the market was only worth a few billion dollars and it said the market default rate for mortgage repayments would be the same for a massive market, doubling every year, as it was for this tiny market. In other words, the data was extrapolated from a very small sample to a much bigger one.

In retrospect, it was a classic error. Another part of the error was the assumption was that an investment could be sold at any time to create solvency. This belief was that money tied up in assets could be turned into cash fast ... but you cannot do that when liquidity disappears, which is why the losses and rescues occurred because banks thought solvent were not. The belief they were solvent was based upon a belief in their asset liquidity, which just wasn't there.

This is due to the alphabet soup of CDOs, CLOs, SIVs, ABS, RMBS, CMBS, and CDS. These instruments all packaged up risk and allowed banks to borrow short and lend long. There's the rub, because if everyone wants their money back, you don't have it, with all of these Structured Investment Vehicles exacerbating it all.

The capital question is also of huge importance to all of us, even though almost no-one took any interest. This is because most people don't understand how banks work.

The Extraordinary Madness of Banks

Under international rules, banks can lend a part of their capital but must keep some back in case it was to the wrong people. The issue with this is that no single issue in bank regulation is more important than this one, and yet no-one knows the answer as to what is the right level of capital a bank must retain.

We've had Basel and Basel II, and still there was a shortage of capital. That shortage is the reason for this crisis. Have you ever heard a politician discuss bank capital before this crisis?

This failure to debate the most basic question in our system has been the core of this crisis. Those basic questions are how much capital should banks hold, and how much capital in total do banks need to retain to cover their total lending?

This is why liquidity was ignored as no-one believed liquidity could just dry up.

And what happens if everyone asks for their money back all at the same time? Especially if those making the request are your counterparties, those who have the major exposures to each other?

That's what the issue was, and this is what caused the biggest run since 1913 on the financial system. It was because liquidity dried up, all the counterparty banks asked for their money back, and many banks just did not have the capital or access to assets for solvency to cover their exposures.

There were other factors but, generally, the false comfort of statistics and maths was a systematic distribution of common sense. This is why people didn't ask the stupid questions such as: if we are lending two to three times the buffers of capital we used to, why? Where's the protection in that?

RBS was leveraged by a factor of 40, and its board thought there was no subprime exposure because they had the illusion of insurance. But their exposure was to insurance, not subprime lenders, which is why they thought this. And the insurers didn't have the resources to make good on subprime loans if the worst happened, so they were taking false comfort too.

The lessons of this crisis are therefore:

- ◆ Don't be in awe of experts;
- ◆ Challenge the science; and
- ◆ Common sense normally trumps statistics.

Who caused this crisis and what's next? (2009)

There are two articles on the ongoing financial crisis debate this week which really caught my eye. The first is in the launch edition of *Wired* magazine for the UK.

The article is entitled: 'Recipe for Disaster: The Formula That Killed Wall Street', and talks about how a young quant analyst at JP Morgan, David X. Li, came up with the formula for de-risking mortgage derivatives in the credit default swaps (CDS) markets and is now the man to blame for this crisis.

Now there have been many names proposed as the instigators of the credit crisis from Alan Greenspan to David Bowie, but David X. Li?

The opening paragraph of the article puts this in context:

"A year ago, it was hardly unthinkable that a math wizard like David X. Li might someday earn a Nobel Prize.

"After all, financial economists – even Wall Street quants – have received the Nobel in economics before, and Li's work on measuring risk has had more impact, more quickly, than previous Nobel Prize-winning contributions to the field.

"Today, though, as dazed bankers, politicians, regulators, and investors survey the wreckage of the biggest financial meltdown since the Great Depression, Li is probably thankful he still has a job in finance at all.

"Not that his achievement should be dismissed. He took a notoriously tough nut – determining correlation, or how seemingly disparate events are related – and cracked it wide open with a simple and elegant mathematical formula, one that would become ubiquitous in finance worldwide."

So what went wrong? This formula, which is known as a 'Gaussian copula function', modelled risk of credit defaults in a way that did not rely on historical data, and became the standard formula for calculating risks in the CDS markets.

The problem with it, as it turned out, is that it was fatally flawed exactly because it did not use real-world data. It had no correlation with the underlying assets, mortgages, and therefore did not work.

However, regulators, ratings agencies, the bond markets and all the trading rooms of the world missed this key feature because it looked so perfect, and used Li's formula to blow up the CDS market from a mere $920 billion in 2001 to a $62 trillion market by the end of 2007.

And that blow up did just that ... blew up. So now everyone blames poor Mr. Li for this crisis. Not so, but Mr. Li's formula certainly is to blame. So, there we go. End of story. Or is it?

The fact is that the explosion has meant a complete degeneration of trust in the financial system and markets as governments haemorrhage budgets to try to fix the issues and consumers wonder how much their houses aren't worth.

So that led me to another magazine, *Prospect*, which this month headlines with an article entitled: 'After Capitalism' by Geoff Mulgan, a director of the Young Foundation.

The sub-heading states: "The era of transition that we are entering will be disruptive – but it may bring a world where markets are servants, not masters", and Mr. Mulgan talks about a wide range of issues and areas behind this crisis and its outcome.

One part really intrigued me:

"To find insights into how the current crisis might connect to these longer-term trends we need to look not to Marx, Keynes or Hayek but to the work of Carlota Perez, a Venezuelan economist whose writings are attracting growing attention.

"Perez is a scholar of the long-term patterns of technological change. In Perez's account economic cycles begin with the emergence of new technologies and infrastructures that promise great wealth; these then fuel frenzies of speculative investment, with dramatic rises in stock and other prices. During these phases finance is in the ascendant and laissez faire policies become the norm. The booms are then followed by dramatic crashes, whether in 1797, 1847, 1893, 1929 or 2008.

"After these crashes, and periods of turmoil, the potential of the new technologies and infrastructures is eventually realised, but only once new institutions come into being which are better aligned with the characteristics of the new economy. Once that has happened, economies then go through surges of growth as well as social progress, like the belle époque or the post-war miracle."

The thesis is one that structures are destroyed by technology and then re-energised into new forms.

The *Economist* sums up Perez's approach in financial innovations:

"Carlota Perez, a Venezuelan economist, thinks that each new industrial technology favours its own sort of financing. Local banks grew up to raise capital for the small companies created in Britain's industrial revolution; joint-stock companies thrived when businessmen needed to finance the railways in the 19th century; industrial banks backed new continental European industries; consumer finance helped Americans buy cars and fridges in the early 20th century. Ms Perez links each financial innovation to its own booms and busts."

I totally buy into the idea that technological revolutions create commercial revolutions create financial revolutions create societal revolutions create political revolutions. Without even knowing of Perez's work, I picked up on this when publishing a paper three years ago on how commercial revolutions create payments revolutions. That is exactly what we are seeing on the back of the networked world.

In fact, although Perez picks up on biotech and life sciences, which will be a revolution, the ramifications of the Wintel, Google, Facebook and related net-based issues have yet to be identified and no-one knows the outcome yet.

But the discussions I'm writing around the future of banking start to point the way to a vision.

Are we there yet? No. And no-one has yet outlined an economic, societal or political vision or an outcome.

My own take would be one based upon community collaboration through citizens' worldwide providing knowledge, skills and expertise through a globally connected pool of talent.

What would that be? Collaborism?

MSNBC rip into Citi and Vikram Pandit (2009)

The piece below from MSNBC is building inflammation on top of inflammation, after seeing the anger over AIG stirred into real anger with this diatribe. I predict a riot. Here's a transcript.

"**Wall Street treated the bailout bill like a national blackmail scheme**

March 19: In a Special Comment, Countdown's Keith Olbermann expresses outrage at Wall Street over their continuing misuse of federal bailout money. Olbermann calls for the firing of bank executives and more stringent bank regulation.

Finally tonight, as promised, a Special Comment on the latest atrocity from the banks. The vast, engorged, gluttonous multinational corporations. Whose sneezes can be fatal to our jobs. Whose mistakes can turn us into the homeless. Whose accounting errors can be so panoramic that they can make our economy tremble and force us to hand them billions after billions in a blackmail scheme that has come to be known as "bailout."

Five weeks ago Vikram Pandit, the chief executive officer of Citigroup, went back to Congress, tail seemingly between his legs, and, with entreaty dripping from his voice, announced "I get the new reality and I'll make sure Citi gets it as well."

In point of fact, as Bloomberg News reports today, what Mr. Pandit "got" was a new $10 million executive suite for himself and his key associates.

This is the same Mr. Pandit who said he would show his leadership by accepting compensation of $1 a year. In fact, he then "accepted" a total compensation package for 2008 of $38 million.

Enough!

Mr. Pandit, you're probably just a good actor and a damned liar and a con man. But I'll give you the benefit of the doubt and assume instead, that you just can't tell the difference between $1 and 38 million of them. That would certainly explain the maelstrom into which you, and your colleagues at Citi and your counterparts elsewhere, have gotten us, including the vast majority of us who are innocent bystanders.

Your bank says your new $10 million office is part of a global strategy of space reduction that will ultimately save billions. It seems entirely appropriate to remind everyone, sir, that this promise could be fulfilled by Citi saving $2 a year for a billion years.

God knows you guys have pulled off every other accounting trick every dreamt up by immoral man. You, sir, and the other

The Extraordinary Madness of Banks

corporate pirates like you – those who are saved from your obsessive spending and greed and self-aggrandizement by the taxpayer – who then pretend to atone – who then publicly promise good behaviour – and who then revert immediately to the rapaciousness that is your only skill.

You, sir, all of you, need to be fired.

Enough!

And Mr. Pandit's corporation should be cut up into little pieces. And when he and the other ultra-millionaires wonder what hit them, we should make sure they are easily reminded. Our representatives should entitle the legislation that ends their moral Ponzi schemes, "The Punish Vikram Pandit Act of 2009."

The far right in this country, without the slightest provocation, screams "socialism," and the sheep who follow it, who do not know what the word means and do not know it is only being used because "communism" now rings laughably hollow. In this cry of fire in a crowded unemployment line, there is outrage.

But there is also licence. They think this is socialism? There is a million miles of reform to go before we hit socialism, but if they're going to call us names whether they apply or not, let's give them real reform.

Break up the banks. Regulate the financial industries, to within an inch of their existences. Roll back corporate legal protections. Make liable the officers of corporations, for their debts, and for their deeds. Resurrect the rallying cry of a hundred years past: bust the trusts!

AIG gives "failure bonuses" to the cretins whose dalliances in derivatives brought the company and part of the nation to her knees? Spin off that division whose traders are owed the 165 million in bonuses, under-fund it, and cause it to go bankrupt.

Enough!

Let those with bonuses owed, stand in line before a bankruptcy referee, and wind up – just as you and I would – with half a cent on the dollar. Northern Trust fires 450 employees in December. Then takes a billion six in bailout money. Sponsors a golf tournament. Flies hundreds of clients to Southern California for private Oscar parties, including the renting of an airplane hangar and the hiring of the group 'Earth, Wind & Fire?'

Enough!

Fire the executives. And fire up the Justice Department to figure out just how much fraud was involved in asking for a billion-six in bailout money when Northern Trust said nothing as the checks were written, even though it knew in advance that millions could be saved by simply cutting the fluff and the trumpery.

Thirteen more companies that took bailouts, signed the mandatory documents that said they owed no back taxes lied turned out, per Congressman John Lewis of Ways and Means today lied – they owe, just among those 13 firms, 220 million in back taxes?

Enough!

Have the IRS take these companies, immediately, to the tax courts to which the rest of us are liable. And strip those ancient, outdated laws of corporation, so that the officers of the corporation are personally liable for their companies' debts, just as you or I would be. And if the monopolies of radio or television rear up to support the corporate structure, to say a contract is a contract, even though that isn't true for a union these days, only for an AIG trader. Take the invisible, unused Sword of Damocles they still fatuously insist hangs over their heads, and make it real.

Enough!

Make sure both sides are heard. Re-regulate the radio and television industries to limit station ownership and demand diversity of management and product. Reinstate the old rules that denied one man all the voices in a public square. End all waivers of multiple ownership of television stations and networks and newspapers in the same market.

The Extraordinary Madness of Banks

And, yes, if a voice of the privileged classes unfairly uses his cable platform to call our neighbours who are the victims of this, "losers", to insist he alone speaks for the real people.

Or if another, indicts without equal time for defence a particular elected official, and then offers himself as a candidate for that very official's seat, in violation of all canons of good or even fair broadcasting then tell the cable industry that the free ride is over and it is time that it too be regulated by the FCC.

Enough!

To all of you in the corporate boardrooms. Stop viewing the public's reaction to this naked, unhindered robbery of the public coffers, and your audacious, immeasurable sense of proprietorship and entitlement, stop viewing our anger as some kind of brief impediment, some traffic delay that keeps you from your God-given corporate ballpark sponsorships, and perpetually remodelled offices, and the divine right of $38 million "compensation packages."

You, gentlemen and ladies, and not the good and long-suffering average people of this country, you are fomenting rage in this nation. You are the losers in this equation, and the people are the generous ones; they have not assembled in the streets with pitch-forks and flaming torches. You are the ones perceived – understood in a visceral and even transcendent way – as the committers of what is becoming class economic rape.

And heed this one word before these people grow weary of forgiving you, and instead decide to bring the "good life" – which you have built on their backs – crashing down on top of your heads. When the next boardroom needs remodelling, or the next bonus paid, or the next jet purchased, remember that one word:

Enough!"

Alan Greenspan caused this crisis (2009)

Back in November 2007, when Alan Greenspan was running around promoting his book, 'The Age of Turbulence', his kudos was high and standing was great. It was just a year after leaving office and subprime had hit, but folks thought it was just a $300 billion hole ... a mere drop in the ocean.

I heard him speak on the public stage back then, and he made many points all of which came back to "It's not my fault".

Now the crisis is a lot bigger with trillions of dollars involved, and many blame Alan Greenspan for it. For example:

- 1987, Alan Greenspan assumed office and total outstanding US home mortgages was $1.82 trillion;
- 1999, total outstanding mortgages in the US was $4.45 trillion;
- 2004, US home mortgages rose to $7.56 trillion; and in 2005, Greenspan's final full year as Fed chairman, home mortgage debt outstanding increased to $9.1 trillion.

In particular, Alan Greenspan was a fan of the free market system and loose self-regulation, as well as a staunch defender of the use of leverage and derivatives to fuel commerce. He now recognises that there was a flaw in that approach, although some would say he could concede such a point when he has made millions out of the free market system personally.

For example, after leaving office, three firms – Deutsche Bank, Hedge Fund Paulson & Co and bond investment company Pacific Investment Management (PIMCO) – hired Alan Greenspan as an adviser on economic issues and monetary policy. Paulson & Co is known for its record $3.7 billion profit making out of the credit crisis, some of which must have flown the Greenspan way.

With Alan Greenspan's bubble burst, everyone now lays the blame at his feet. This is clearly demonstrated by the media and

41

online rants and raves, with the latest to prompt such outcry coming from two UK newspapers that ran a poll this week to find out who we all think is to blame for this crisis. Alan Greenspan comes out #1 in both. Equally, in a US poll by the *Institutional Investor*, those who should know, 53% blame Greenspan, 28% George W. Bush and, interestingly, 16% Bill Clinton.

What such polls serve to achieve I have no idea, but it does show that Mr. Greenspan might be advised to avoid walking down the street on his own at night for a while.

CDS doom and gloom (2008)

Wolfgang Munchau writes in the *Financial Times* today that the issues we faced in subprime in 2007 are just a mere drop in the ocean, and that this is more than just a subprime crisis:

> "If this had been a mere subprime crisis, it would now be over. But it is not, and nor will it be over soon. The reason is that several other pockets of the credit market are also vulnerable. Credit cards are one such segment, similar in size to the subprime market. Another is credit default swaps, relatively modern financial instruments that allow bondholders to insure against default."

Let's take the credit card area first. According to the *Guardian*, "America's card debt is around $900bn compared with a relatively modest £56bn in Britain." However, the UK actually has similar levels of exposure per capita. Peter Farley, Managing Director of Financial Insights Europe, last year when he presented at the Financial Services Club said: "We have reached a position where personal debt in the UK has risen to a total of £1,291 billion at the end of 2006, more than 10% higher than a year earlier and nearly triple the level it stood at 10 years ago."

So, we should be worried about the personal credit market collapsing although the real concern, according to Mr. Munchau, is the total risk exposure in Credit Default Swap (CDS) derivatives.

A year ago, I stated a little around this issue in discussing the quest for alpha and noting that "hedge funds account for 32% of credit default swap sellers and 28% of buyers, up from 15% and 16% in2004". But the real base of this concern goes back to trading strategies, which I discussed back in April 2006. That discussion was focused upon trading strategies and algo systems and, since then, we've seen several market movements to create additional market risk.

So, what's the problem with CDS? Well, the way these systems work is like an insurance policy for a bank's credit risk. Banks take a basket of loans, and then offer the option to cover these loans if they default to investors. The investor only has to pay if the loan defaults. If the loan is paid off, then the investor wins as they keep all the premiums the bank has paid them.

This is fine in times of a boom, as there are virtually no insolvencies. However, during a recessionary period, insolvencies rise and kaboom! Bang goes CDS derivatives and we have a major market explosion.

Now we all recognise that there are market and credit risks in the financial world, but we manage them. What Mr. Munchau's column raises in my mind is the question of whether there is a systemic risk in the markets?

Have all of our debt-based tools and instruments created a systemic market risk which could bring down the financial markets worldwide?

Certainly, our debt instruments are untested. That is why Warren Buffett calls derivatives "weapons of financial destruction". Certainly, subprime has been a problem and, if CDS derivatives explode too, then we do have a major issue.

The Extraordinary Madness of Banks

Mr. Munchau's contention is that these instruments have not been tested during a major recession and, if the USA enters a recession, then the markets could implode.

Let's have a think about this, then.

America has enjoyed a boom period for the past half century, much of it fuelled by manufacturing and technological innovations. As a result, the dollar has been the world's globally trusted currency and America has used this strength to leverage debt. However, this has changed as, in more recent times, some of the American economy has been fuelled by consumer demand and government borrowing, based upon a strong dollar and driven by debt.

This is all fine in periods of boom where America has strength but, with the dollar weak, inflation on the horizon and a recession looming, Mr. Munchau's contention is that we should be worried. Especially if this recession is a deep and long one – of the sort not seen since the mid-1970s – as this would test the financial markets like they've never been tested before. After all, 30 years ago we did not have the multi-trillion exposures created by debt-based derivatives and credit-based products. As a result, the fact these products will be tested for the first time in 2008 should be cause for concern.

Mr. Munchau also cites a report produced last week by Bill Gross of Pimco, which roughly calculates loss exposures in CDS derivatives to be around $250 billion. Add that to the $400 billion plus in subprime losses, along with a tasty little credit card crisis, and you can see why he's worried.

However, one thing he fails to mention is the strength of sovereign wealth funds (SWF) in China, India and the Middle East and elsewhere. Therefore, maybe we are actually seeing a balance shift in capital ownership. In addition, you always have two sides of the coin, a little like Alan Greenspan's gloomy view of the world versus Steve Forbes.

Are the doomsayers being far too pessimistic? We shall see.

CDOs created this crisis (2007)

There's a saying that "When you see a way of making money with no risks, you see the fool's gold", I guess the obvious question is: why didn't the banks see the fool's gold? After all, these are institutions that go back over five centuries, with departments that deal with market risk, credit risk, operational risk and have advanced risk measurement systems.

It is reasonable to ask whether it was bank policy to write the loans and hope to profit from the capital appreciation on fore-closure, or whether the incentives for the brokers were such that they did not care about the credit quality?

So here's my take on it. The current crisis is mainly related to the latter and, to a great extent, the spread of and widespread usage of CDOs which hid the risks. That's why the banks didn't see the fool's gold.

CDOs – Collateralised Debt Obligations – allowed banks to take on higher risk lending strategies because they could get rid of the risk to other banks and corporates. A paper was written in depth on this area by Joseph Mason, an associate finance professor at Drexel University's business school, and Joshua Rosner, a managing director at research firm Graham Fisher & Co. The paper, titled 'How Resilient Are Mortgage Backed Securities to Collateralized Debt Obligation Market Disruptions?', came out in February and has some interesting stats on this market showing that the growth of CDOs has been explosive. In 1995, there were hardly any rising to more than $500 billion by 2006 of which 40% were backed by residential mortgage and almost three quarters of those were in subprime.

CDOs allowed the banks to lay off more risk to others, and were created specifically as a complex credit derivative to allow greater lending liquidity. As a result, banks could lend excessively and relax their credit risk control measures to a large extent by laying off the risks to other banks and corporates through CDOs.

The fact that these risks were minimised through collateral – a house – that was worth more than the loans meant there was no problem ... apart from a housing price boom that didn't exist and was fuelled by such lending practices.

This is fool's folly and now we're seeing the consequences. **And we have seen it all before.** I mean, it rings bells with me going back to America's thrift crisis of the 1980s. There's a report from 2003 looking exactly at the systemic risks in the US mortgage markets and how to avoid this (fat lot of good that did).

But there are also solutions from those who did learn their lessons and, for me, this crisis has most similarity with the Lloyd's of London insurance losses in the 1980s. That crisis almost meant the closure of a marketplace that had existed since the 17th century ... ring any bells with where I started?

What was that crisis all about? Exactly the same as today's issue ... just with different nuances. The Lloyd's crisis began because they took on more and more risk during the early 1980s and thought they had it covered.

The Lloyd's underwriting syndicates took on the risks because they could lay off the risk to external organisations which reinsure and cover the exposure. Eventually, at the top of the tree, you had an excess of loss syndicate which covered the greatest exposures if there were ever disasters.

The thing is, there were rarely any disasters of the magnitude that affected those excess of loss firms. As a result, those excess of loss firms were the most profitable Lloyd's syndicates because they never had to pay out any claims. Therefore the names joined those excess of loss syndicates and the Lloyd's desks took on more and more risk.

Then it all went wrong and Lloyd's almost went bust. What happened? This is quite complicated but relates to our markets today very strongly.

The way Lloyd's excess of loss worked was that you might have an oil rig or property development worth $1 billion. That's a huge risk policy so the firm would go to Lloyd's to get the cover as Lloyd's specialised in it.

The client would go to an underwriter, and ask to get $1 billion of cover and the underwriter would happily take this on because they could lay off the risk. They would lay off $900 million of that risk to reinsurance firms **outside** the Lloyd's markets, so it was no problem. The trouble was that the reinsurer laid off their risk to another Lloyd's syndicate, and so $750 million of the risk came back **into** Lloyd's. Therefore, the total risk to Lloyd's was $850 million: $100 million with the first syndicate and $750 with the second. Lloyd's troubles started there, as we shall see later, as they thought they just had $100 million of exposure.

The cycle would probably go round once more, with $600 million of the $750 million of the second syndicate being reinsured outside Lloyd's. Then the reinsurer comes back into Lloyd's and places $400 million with an excess of loss firm. This excess of loss firm was happy to take that last $400 million because they never had to pay. Bear in mind, it would have to be a total disaster to pay out the $1 billion and, even if there was a disaster, the first $600 million of risk was covered by the others. That's why excess of loss firms were always profitable.

But then the disasters hit. Asbestosis and pollution claims, combined with natural disasters like Hurricane Betsy and Piper Alpha, meant that Lloyd's total risk exposure was impacted. You suddenly had reinsurance firms paying out $350 million, and Lloyd's paying out $650 million of which $400 was with the final desk, the excess of loss desk.

Lloyd's never knew that would happen because every time the risk was reinsured outside the Lloyd's markets, they thought they had got rid of it. So what they thought they had exposed themselves to was $100 million here, $150 million there and $400 million at the end of the game on another deal that was unlikely to ever be paid. Suddenly, they realised they were up for $650 million for a single incident!

The excess of loss firms also banked on rarely having to pay a claim and, if they did, it would be once in a blue moon. After all, **total** disasters rarely happen.

Then several total disasters all happened at once, and so the $650 million exposure was not just for one or two risks, but for several that overlapped and were inter-related. In other words, Lloyd's exposures due to these disasters meant that one market was covering virtually the whole world's risks. That's an awful lot for a small market, and almost meant the market collapsed.

But Lloyd's got through it. A few syndicates collapsed. Others learnt their lessons and now have systems that look at risk across the whole market, rather than on an exposure by exposure basis.

Banks will do the same ... eventually.

So going back to where I started: why didn't banks see the fool's gold? It was because, as with the total risk on a single policy at Lloyd's, the fool's gold was hidden.

CDOs combined with CDS and other exotic derivatives meant that, like Lloyd's in the 1980s, the risk got moved out and then back in. It got moved out of the bank through their investment desk's derivatives operations and moved back into the bank by allowing them to take on huge mortgage debt risk.

The problem for tomorrow will be: how will the banks ever get to the stage of seeing the total risk across all of the markets and all of their operations?

How accountable are the rating agencies for this mess? (2009)

We all talk about how the rating agencies were, in part, responsible for creating the mess of credit and credit instruments that caused this crisis.

After all, they are meant to be rating credit, aren't they?

But I didn't realise exactly how bad a job these guys had done until I saw this quote:

> "In January 2008, there were 12 AAA-rated companies in the world. At the same time, there were 64,000 structured finance instruments, such as CDOs, rated AAA."

Lloyd Blankfein, Chairman and Chief Executive of Goldman Sachs, Speech to the Council of Institutional Investors, April 2009

Jeez ... now we know.

Chapter 2 Governments in action

The
**Complete
Banker**

Introduction

Following the implosion of the global financial markets, governments rallied together rapidly to try to work out what happened, why, and what to do about it. It was quite sad to watch, really, as many of the governmental players were the same people who created the conditions for the crisis. For example, UK Prime Minister Gordon Brown claimed to be decisive after the failure of Northern Rock, the sudden merger of Lloyds and HBOS and the bailing-out of RBS. However, it was his own actions as Chancellor that allowed the irrational mortgage lending practices of these banks to take place. Similarly in the USA, Alan Greenspan, who ran the Federal Reserve Bank policymaking that led to the sub-prime markets, denied any responsibility for months after the crisis hit, only to eventually realise that it was his total belief in free market practices that had failed. Therefore, when we wonder about the causes of this crisis, much lies firmly at the feet of politicians and policymakers, as they are in charge of the controls that keep markets in check or allow them to fly free and unfettered.

What is this f****r fee? (2010)

So yesterday's big news is the new Financial Crisis Responsibility Fee, the FCR, or f****r fee, as the bankers are calling it. This is Obama's big idea to get back lost TARP funds, by introducing a tax of $1.5 million per billion dollars of liabilities on a bank's balance sheet.

The aim is to raise $117 billion to make up for the losses during the financial crisis. The way it will work is that the banks pay this 0.15% on liabilities and, according to Goldman Sachs, there are around $5.5 trillion of liabilities on American banks' balance sheets, so that's around $8 billion per year. The tax will apply for 10 years, until 2020, or until the TARP fund losses are repaid.

The fee will be applied to only the largest banks, those with more than $50 billion worth of assets, and 60% of the tax will be paid for by the largest banks: JPMorgan, Citi, Bank of America, Wells Fargo, Goldman and co. In fact, the biggest banks will be paying about $2 billion a year for this tax.

There's also about $1 billion a year that will be paid by UK banks Royal Bank of Scotland (which owns Citizens and Charter One Banks), HSBC (which owns Household) and Barclays (which bought the US operations of Lehmans).

Sounds bad, but it's not so bad. US banks made $250 billion in earnings last year, so paying back up to $10 billion a year in tax ain't so bad. In fact, I was amazed to find a figure that states that Goldman Sachs made $100 million a day in earnings last year every day for over 200 trading days. So a billion here or there in taxes ain't so bad, especially if you're paying billions in bonuses and annoying everyone.

The FCR fee is stirring stuff therefore, and very populist as it ensures that Barack Obama "recovers every single dime the American people are owed", and hits at the heart of the anger everyone has with bankers making "massive profits and obscene bonuses".

In some ways, it's a good idea. It targets leverage and borrowings that banks tap into in the wholesale markets, which is where Lehman and Northern Rock got scuppered and where Goldman Sachs and Morgan Stanley plough their trough.

The FCR fee also positions itself as the insurance fee which the banks should have paid to get themselves bailed out. They didn't pay any insurance but then found they were too big to fail so the Fed insured them. This is now payback time.

But it won't work. First, it hits at the banks, but the banks have paid back TARP. $165 billion of TARP funds were repaid by US banks last year, with an average return to the US taxpayer of an 8% yield. That's why the Fed made a $45 billion profit last year, through bond purchases and interest on the emergency loans made to financial institutions. It was General Motors, Chrysler and AIG that lost the $120 billion of funds that Obama wants to recoup.

Second, the banks will just pass on the cost of the tax to their customers and investors. Jamie Dimon, CEO of JPMorgan, made the comment straight off that "all businesses pass costs on to customers", and it is highly likely that the banks will find some way to hide this tax in the costs of doing business. The result is that the proposed tax will be rejected by Congress, which sees any tax on the taxpayer as being untenable. The tax has to be directly on the bank.

Third, Geithner ruled out a Tobin tax on bank transactions at the G20 Finance Ministers summit in Gleneagles last November for the reasons outlined in point two above. The trouble is that the FCR fee is a variation of a Tobin tax and needs to be better thought out. Obama had and has until 2013 to find a way to get the lost TARP funds repaid, and so he doesn't need to do something this fast or ill-conceived.

Finally, this does not address the two biggest issues: bankers' bonuses and being too big to fail. Obama claims it gets at "massive profits and obscene bonuses" ... how? I don't see it.

If these are the major issues that lie at the heart of the post-crisis bubble of media and public bile, then these need to be addressed, but the FCR fee doesn't do it. The FCR fee purely repays TARP.

In fact, if bonuses and too big to fail are the core issues then these issues need to be addressed through a G20 agenda, not a unilateralist position, whether it be in the UK, USA, France or elsewhere.

Therefore, it is far more likely that the FCR fee will be rejected by Congress and Geithner and Obama end up working with Barnier, Darling, Brown, Sarkozy and company on clawbacks and

54

taxes on banker's bonuses, along with a variation of Glass-Steagall to bring back a return to 'narrow banking'. In other words, split the risky investment markets from the retail depositors.

This last point is the key act forecast to happen over the next year or so, and is far more likely to be operable and implementable than a FCR fee.

Gordon Brown's entente cordiale

Much has been made today of the fact that Gordon Brown and Nicolas Sarkozy have jointly written an opinion piece in the *Wall Street Journal*. Here are some highlights from their article:

"The way global financial institutions have operated raises fundamental questions that we must – and can only – address globally.

"We have found that a huge and opaque global trading network involving complex products, short-termism and too-often excessive rewards created risks that few people understood. We have also learned that when crises happen, taxpayers have to cover the costs. It is simply not acceptable for them to foot the bill for losses in a deep downturn, while institutions' shareholders and employees enjoy all the gains as the economy recovers.

"Better regulation and supervision are the means by which the risk to the taxpayer can be reduced for the longer term ...

"There is an urgent need for a new compact between global banks and the society they serve.

"A compact that recognizes the risks to the taxpayer if banks fail and recognises the imbalance between risks and rewards in the banking system.

The Extraordinary Madness of Banks

"A compact that ensures the benefits of good economic times flow not just to bankers but to the people they serve; that makes sure that the financial sector fosters economic growth.

"A compact that ensures financial institutions cannot use off-shore tax havens to negate the contribution they justly owe to the citizens of the country in which they operate – and so builds on the progress already made in ending tax and regulatory havens.

"Therefore, we propose a long-term global compact that will encapsulate both the responsibilities of the banking system and the risk they pose to the economy as a whole. Various proposals have been put forward and deserve examination. They include resolution funds, insurance premiums, financial transaction levies and a tax on bonuses.

"Among these proposals, we agree that a one-off tax in relation to bonuses should be considered a priority, due to the fact that bonuses for 2009 have arisen partly because of government support for the banking system.

"However, it is clear the action that must be taken must be at a global level. No one territory can be expected to or be able to act on its own."

Hmmm ... in yesterday's pre-budget announcement the UK Treasury leader Alistair Darling announced a unilateral 50% tax on any bonuses over £25,000 with immediate effect.

First, the banks will find a way around such a tax. Second, there's already a 50% tax rate on earnings over £150,000, so big deal. Third, what's the point of unilaterally taxing bankers if other nations, especially the US, don't do this, as it will just mean that bankers move to other financial centres to work.

Aha. So that's why Gordon Brown has written an article in the *Wall Street Journal* – a US financial paper – avec M. Sarkozy who will naturally be supportive as his lead Finance Minister, Christine Lagarde, has been fighting this corner for a while. The aim being to show a united European approach and place pressure on Barack Obama to follow suit, as discussed in the *New Yorker* (see 'Will Obama tax the Banksters?').

Add all this up with the sweetener that the new head of financial regulation in Brussels, Michel Barnier, is Sarkozy's lieutenant and maybe this all explains why Mr. Brown is cosying up to the French.

Je comprend maintenant.

Gordon Brown's Tobin tax ... duh? (2009)

Many of us thought it a bit weird that Gordon Brown suggested bringing back the Tobin tax last weekend during the G20 summit. The idea is to tax every financial transaction, just a little bit, one or two cents on each ... this way you can build up a fund for any future financial shocks.

The reason it's a bit weird is that any action by governments need to be co-ordinated across all G20 nations – unilateral activities will just cause banks to relocate elsewhere – and Gordon had zero support for this idea from his usually supportive key allies.

As with the bank bonuses debate, the issue of unilateral versus collective responsibility is a big concern and is why the UK and USA have been acting in close harmony, like Siamese twins, during this crisis to make sure they're co-ordinated in all announcements.

So it was very strange that Brown would suggest the Tobin tax when Tim Geithner came out five minutes later, saying that it was not something the US would consider.

The Extraordinary Madness of Banks

But what was even weirder, as pointed out by *Private Eye* this week, is that the government and Gordon Brown have consistently rejected the idea of a Tobin tax for the past decade.

For example, in May 2002 when Gordon Brown was Chancellor, he made this statement to the Parliamentary Committee for International Development:

> "The problem is that each of the other proposals, like the Tobin tax ... has very substantial drawbacks and they have failed to command the international support that is necessary for us to raise the level of finance over a short period of time so that we can achieve the Millennium Development Goals."

The rich vein of anti-Tobin views continues through the ensuing years as, just last December, Gordon Brown was asked in Prime Minister's Questions whether he would support such a tax:

> "There are many proposals to deal with the reform of international financial institutions to make them more able to deal with the problems that the world faces, not just the financial stability problems, but climate change. One such proposal is the Tobin tax, which has been found by many people who have looked at it not to be implementable."

Even in August, when Lord Turner of the FSA mentioned the idea, it was pooh-poohed by the Chancellor. Nevertheless, this was the same dialogue by Lord Turner where he used the phrase "socially useless". Ever since, we've all been wondering what role for the future for banks in society, and the idea of bringing back the Tobin tax on financial transactions has obviously seeped into Brown's armoury.

So maybe Lord Turner has convinced him to make a U-turn on Britain's anti-Tobin tax feelings. Now, there's no reason why a politician shouldn't do a U-turn. It doesn't look good but, bear in mind that back in 2002-2003, Gordon Brown also refused to believe there was a credit bubble burgeoning in Britain.

(...)

Times have changed and obviously Gordon Brown is not a soothsayer or Nostradamus or Warren Buffett ... and so he might be right in performing a U-turn on this tax on transactions. The only mistake he made was not running this past the Americans (and Canadians, Russians and IMF) beforehand as they all rejected it out of hand, as he probably knew they would.

If you ask me it was just a cunning plan, to get more support for Tony Blair in the new EU roles of European President. After all, the Tobin tax is specifically supported and promoted by the French and Germans. Showing support of their policies may well be a political play that Gordon thought a good one.

Maybe Gordon Brown is Hu Jintao (2009)

Not accusing Gordon Brown of being Chinese or anything except that, in the context of banking, he does seem to have taken a leaf out of the book of the Chinese leadership of Hu Jintao.

China's answer to the economic meltdown is to tell the banks to lend, no matter what the costs or risks, with new lending jumping 1000% in December as rules on loans to deposits ratios were eased.

Now that's not what the government here is saying, but it does want the banks to return to lending. That is why the UK government is to offer banks guarantees on existing loans to the value of possibly £200 billion ($300 billion) to try to get new lending started again. Rather than a Septic Bank, we're creating a Toxic Insurance Firm.

The headlines of the announcement are likely to be:

◆ The ability to move toxic assets off the bank balance sheets through an insurance scheme to guarantee payments against such assets;
◆ Guarantees on new consumer loans;
◆ Softening the terms of £37 billion recapitalisation of Royal Bank of Scotland (RBS), Lloyds TSB and HBOS last October.

The last point is an interesting one. Last October, £9 billion ($13.5 billion) of the £37 billion ($50 billion) provided by the government for the banks' recapitalisation, was in the form of preference shares charged at 12% interest.

Now, banks will be offered the chance to convert these preference shares into ordinary shares, reducing the interest rate charged to a more reasonable 5% or thereabouts, but increasing the government's equity stake by the same token. In the case of RBS, this nationalises the bank even further as the government's stake would increase from being 57.9% state-owned to 70%, and now with voting rights too.

A quick round-robin of the Sunday newspapers:

The Times: 'You can't fast-track a financial meltdown': "The government is expected to underwrite toxic assets on the balance sheets of Britain's beleaguered banks – a move designed to enable banks to start lending again. We would all like to think it is the final act required to start turning round our economy. Think again. Against a backdrop of fear about the scale of the toxic assets held within banks and the denial, this could end up being another sticking-plaster initiative."

The *Independent*: 'Taxpayers could be liable for £200bn in toxic bank loans': "The 'safety net' proposal, being hammered out by the Prime Minister, the Chancellor, Alistair Darling, and bank bosses, would require institutions to identify their most troublesome loans and pay into a state-sponsored insurance scheme. Although the liabilities would still be owned by the banks, taxpayers would ultimately have to pick up the tab for losses greater than an agreed amount."

Meanwhile the *Sunday Telegraph*, the Conservative's paper, went to town on the whole debacle: '£200bn to save banks from bad debt': "The taxpayer will be forced to underwrite up to £200 billion of bad banking debt under a government plan to take control of assets belonging to Britain's major high street lenders, The *Daily Telegraph* can disclose ... that equates to about £33,000 per taxpayer."

'Taxpayers face years of debt in bank salvage deal': "Were taxpayers to directly acquire the banks' worst assets, one of the major problems would have been valuing them. The insurance scheme puts less pressure on the government and banks to strike a price for toxic assets. Lenders would keep their bad debts on their books but they would be underwritten by the taxpayer."

'80 per cent of bank lending "went overseas"': "Britain's banks are facing a rising tide of government anger after it emerged that up to 80 per cent of their lending has been to overseas borrowers"

The last point is particularly going to create an irate storm amongst the politicians and public, as it is this uncovering of toxic debt to predominantly overseas firms that apparently sparked Gordon Brown's anger, and the need for another major bailout plan.

A government source said: "It was pretty breathtaking to discover these figures. They provide further evidence that so many of the problems we are all facing started with bad banking practice on the international markets and were not simply caused by problems with the British economy."

So the UK taxpayer is left with the debt of foreign firms and individuals caused by banks' irrational growth plans fuelled through leveraged lending.

No wonder Ed Miliband, the government's Climate Secretary, made a speech to the Fabian Society saying that: "This is no ordinary time because, in the same way that September 11 shook the foundations of a thesis about foreign policy ... so the economic events we have witnessed have done the same to our domestic politics."

The banking system collapse is as crippling as the 9/11 terrorist attacks on the World Trade Centre? Strong words, but maybe not far off the mark.

What it really means is that the government needs to become far more of an 'activist investor' in the banking system, and tell the banks' management teams what actions to take.

This is true in China and the USA. For example, interesting article over at Caller.com that says the US government is already starting to flex muscles, after telling Vikram Pandit to restructure and breakup Citigroup.

Charles Elson, director of the Weinberg Center for Corporate Governance at University of Delaware, is quoted: "When the government says move, banks have to move. The government trumps any decision coming from management or the board."

Too right!

Result: Gordon Brown and Alastair Darling will tell the banks to lend, just as Hu Jintao has in China.

The Feng Shui is written on the wall, and I have seen one economist forecast that Britain will go cap-in-hand to the International Monetary Fund this year ... we shall see.

The end of the American dream (2008)

I guess we all need a good joke right now, and I thought the vote down of the rescue plan for America's financial system was a joke last night.

Then I found out it was true! The Bailout Bill was rejected, and left America's rescue dream in tatters.

Was it because the Bill would not work? Maybe, as the UK government has spent over $200 billion bailing out Bradford & Bingley and Northern Rock, just two banks. So will $700 billion cover the whole US banking system and its problems? Maybe not.

But that's not why it failed to go through. It failed because some Republicans allegedly blame Nancy Pelosi, the Speaker of the House, and a Democrat. Her speech before the Bill vote was viewed as far too partisan. Just 12 votes separated a win from a loss. 228 votes to 205. 12 Republican votes made the difference, even though, by doing so, she and the other politicos have completely blown out any American credibility in financial markets ... but some would say they blew that credibility away a while ago, with the mismanagement of the markets that led to this crisis.

Is this the end of the American dream? Seems to be ... until the next vote. Is this the end of America's global dominance? Absolutely.

Now I am not anti-American. I love America and much of what it stands for. However, as the BBC reported, the politicians were running frightened as there is an election in five weeks, and so "rejected a bill which the Treasury and the Federal Reserve had insisted was essential to the stability and viability of the American financial system – and by extension the financial system of the entire world."

Have they killed the world's financial system? No. But they have seriously infected it and need to find an antidote fast.

But that's not why they have broken the American dream. What was broken yesterday is the 'rose-tinted glasses' through which the rest of the world has viewed America. Those glasses were smudged by the Iraq war, fogged by the subprime crisis and broken by the last two weeks mess of indecision.

America lost a lot of kudos, goodwill and support as a result of the Iraq War, but it had not diminished America's economic and financial dominance. The inter-linkage of all economies is to the global currency reserve of the dollar, for example, and that is still the case. Until yesterday.

America equally has led the world in believing that financial leverage creates growth creates commerce creates GDP creates wealth creates leverage … until yesterday.

America has also led the investment markets thanks to Lehman Brothers, Merrill Lynch, Goldman Sachs and Morgan Stanley. Until now.

This is because America created a toxic recipe under the Alan Greenspan years where greed, globalisation, technology and regulation combined to shatter the American dream. These ingredients were all placed in a melting pot and what came out was a complex soup of derivatives, which are now unravelling. Collateralised Debt Obligations (CDO), Credit Default Swaps (CDS), Structured Investment Vehicles (SIV) and their kindred have blown the American dream to pieces.

You only need to look at the charts on the BBC's website to see the killer combination and timing that led to yesterday's vote in the House of Representatives. Interestingly, an American colleague described the BBC as 'far too liberal', but then we are run by Labour (the Democrats equivalent) rather than the Liberals.

The BBC does make an incisive comment, however, that American voters perceive Wall Street bankers to be "greedy, incompetent fat cats who have created this crisis themselves and who are now being allowed to pick the pockets of American voters to fix it."

That's why the Republicans voted it down. There's an election in five weeks and they are running scared of being voted out of office. None of this is new though. Not the political self-interest, or these boom and bust cycles. The causes of this crisis are not new either. It all lies with structured finance, leverage and complex derivatives.

But today I raise my glass, hang my head and lift my hat to the end of the American dream.

The dream was damaged by war, ravaged by money and assassinated by political self-interest. It's not Democrats versus Republicans right now, but possibly America versus the Rest of the World. America, I think the political self-interests of all your politicians killed the American dream yesterday. You also pulled the rug on the little bit of credibility you might have had left.

Back to the jokes. Apparently, a major investment was made yesterday in Pfizer's stocks by 12 Republicans as they wanted to ensure they had a little bit of help in the next five weeks to get a stronger election.

It didn't work.

Why the G20 will disagree with the IMF reforms (2010)

I don't know if any of you read the IMF report recommending two new bank taxes:

◆ A bank levy based upon the risk banks represent, called a Financial Stability Contribution (FSC); and
◆ A straight tax on profits and bonuses called the Financial Activities Tax (FAT).

If you haven't, then I can recommend it's worth a skim. For example, they reject the Tobin tax / Robin Hood tax idea, saying that this would just get passed on to customers by the banks.

However, the fact that they support the idea of a levy and a tax – a double whammy – could have bankers worried ... except that bankers are pretty clever at tax avoidance and Canada and Japan have said they won't implement these plans so it's a G18 agreement right now, or less.

In my view, the document is also flawed. Here's why.

The document itself is just for discussion for the G20 Ministers meeting this week, with the aim of agreeing something in June. But it does contain some really interesting appendices which are noteworthy as useful research materials, covering diverse subjects from each country's proposals for reform to their contributions to the bank crisis to date.

For example, the table opposite shows the amounts announced or pledged for financial sector support so far, as a percentage of 2009's GDP.

	Capital Injection	Purchase of Assets and Lending by Treasury	Direct Support	Guarantees	Asset Swap and Purchase of Financial Assets, including Treasuries, by Central Bank	Upfront Government Financing
	(A)	(B)	(A+B)	(C)	(D)	(E)
G-20 Average	**2.6**	**1.4**	**4.0**	**6.4**	**4.6**	**3.1**
Advanced Economies	3.8	2.4	6.2	13.2	7.7	5.0
in billions of US$	1,220	756	1,976	3.530	2.400	1,610
Emerging Economies	0.7	0.1	0.8	16.9	0.0	0.2
in billions of US$	90	18	108	7	0	24

The Extraordinary Madness of Banks

What this shows is that for the 'advanced economies' – think USA, UK, France, Germany, Japan et al – the cost has been 6.2% of GDP in direct support and a further 10.9% in guarantees. The total of columns A to E represents 29.8% of advanced economies' GDP in 2009. That compares with 1.8% in the emerging economies – think the BRICs, Indonesia, et al.

Mind you, they then go on to say that "for the advanced G-20 economies, the average amount utilized for capital injection was 2 percent of GDP, that is $639 billion, or just over half the pledged amounts. France, Germany, the USA and the UK accounted for over 90 percent of this. For the advanced G-20 economies, the utilized amount for asset purchases was around 1.4 percent of GDP, less than two-thirds of the pledged amount. Similarly, the uptake of guarantees has been markedly less than pledged."

This is why the report reckons that the global financial crisis has cost about $533 billion less than originally estimated, and is now just a mere $2.28 trillion when all is said and done.

Now, who's the daddy when it comes to global bailouts and guarantees? Have a look at the table opposite.

	Capital Injection	Purchase of Assets and Lending by Treasury 2/	Direct Support 3/	Guarantees 4/	Asset Swap and Purchase of Financial Assets, including Treasuries, by Central Bank	Upfront Government Financing 5/
	(A)	(B)	(A+B)	(C)	(D)	(E)
Advanced Economies						
Australia	0.0	0.0	0.0	13.2	0.0	0.0
Canada	0.0	9.1	9.1	0.0	0.0	9.1
France	1.3	0.2	1.5	16.9	0.0	1.1
Germany	3.4	0.0	3.4	17.2	0.0	3.4
Italy	1.3	0.0	1.3	0.0	2.7	2.7
Japan	2.5	4.1	6.6	7.2	0.0	0.4
Korea	1.2	1.5	2.7	11.6	0.0	0.8
United Kingdom	8.2	3.7	11.9	40.0	28.2	8.7
United States	5.1	2.3	7.4	7.5	12.1	7.4

The Extraordinary Madness of Banks

Wow, the UK wins! We're number one, we're number one, we're number one, woohoohoo!.

Wait a minute. That means we're #1 in global bailouts of banks. Hmmm ... not sure if we should be so thrilled with that accolade and maybe this is why Gordon Brown is so keen on the idea of a Tobin tax or a Robin Hood tax or a Financial Activities tax or ... well, any tax really to help with our debt mountain, to be honest. The burden of national debt amongst the G7 nations is at a 60-year high, with the UK's Treasury planning to increase national debt by over £560 billion between now and 2015. That's about $800 billion or almost a trillion.

Meanwhile, the emerging economies paint a very different picture, as shown in the table opposite.

2 : Governments in action

	Capital Injection	Purchase of Assets and Lending by Treasury 2/	Direct Support 3/	Guarantees 4/	Asset Swap and Purchase of Financial Assets, including Treasuries, by Central Bank	Upfront Government Financing 5/
	(A)	(B)	(A+B)	(C)	(D)	(E)
Emerging Economies						
Argentina	0.0	0.0	0.0	0.0	0.0	0.0
Brazil	0.0	0.8	0.0	0.5	0.0	0.0
China	0.0	0.0	0.0	0.0	0.0	0.0
India	0.0	0.0	0.0	0.0	0.0	0.0
Indonesia	0.0	0.0	0.0	0.0	0.0	0.0
Mexico	0.0	0.0	0.0	0.0	0.0	0.0
Russia	7.1	0.5	7.7	0.0	0.0	1.9
Saudi Arabia	0.0	0.0	0.0	0.0	0.0	0.0
South Africa	0.0	0.0	0.0	0.0	0.0	0.0
Turkey	0.0	0.0	0.0	0.0	0.0	0.0

The Extraordinary Madness of Banks

Apart from Russia, this crisis has cost the key future economies of the world urrmmmm ... nothing.

These charts make it clear that **nine** of the G20 nations have had no crisis. Add to this the fact that Canada's financial system has been the most stable in the world, and Japan does not intend to implement these tax and levy options, and you realise that under half of the G20 will be keen to support any radical changes to the financial markets.

It's not as clear-cut as this, as the fact that the advanced economies' bailouts allowed the emerging economies to survive this crisis without their economies also imploding is a key part of the dialogue.

Another useful chart (see opposite) shows why the IMF has reduced the bailout numbers by $533 billion where financial markets have used far less of the pledged amounts than those offered by their respective governments:

	Capital Injection		Purchase of Assets and Lending by Treasury 2/	
	Amount used	In percent of announce-ment	Amount used	In percent of announce-ment
Advanced Economies				
Australia	0.0	...	0.0	...
Canada	0.0	...	83.2	48.4
France	1.1	83.2	0.0	0.0
Germany	1.2	35.0	83.2	...
Italy	0.3	20.3	0.0	...
Japan	0.1	2.4	0.1	1.4
Korea	0.4	32.5	0.1	3.8
United Kingdom	6.4	78.5	0.1	4.0
United States	2.9	57.0	1.9	84.0
Emerging Economies				
Argentina	0.0	...	0.0	...
Brazil	0.0	...	0.3	43.5
China	0.0	...	0.0	...
India	0.0	...	0.0	...
Indonesia	0.0	...	0.0	...
Mexico	0.0	...	0.0	...
Russia	3.1	43.0	0.0	0.0
Saudi Arabia	0.0	...	0.0	...
South Africa	0.0	...	0.0	...
Turkey	0.0	...	0.0	...
G-20 Average	1.3	51.7	0.9	60.2
Advanced Economies	2.0	52.3	1.4	61.0
in billions of US$	639	...	461	...
Emerging Economies	0.3	43.0	0.03	27.5
in billions of US$	38.4	...	5.0	...

The Extraordinary Madness of Banks

Finally, these charts are followed by a review of each country's bank taxation policies implemented or proposed (Appendix 2, Page 32), a review of corrective taxation and prudential policies (Appendix 3) and the current taxation policies (Appendix 4).

This last section is also particularly intriguing as it demonstrates why banking has been so critical to Gordon Brown's policies of the past decade. For example, here's the percentage of a country's total tax pool raised from financial firms by country.

G20 corporate taxes paid by the financial sector (%)

	Period	Share of Corporate Taxes	Share of Total Tax Revenue
Argentina	2006 – 2008	6.0	1.0
Australia	FY2007	15.0	2.8
Brazil	2006 – 2008	15.4	1.8
Canada	2006 – 2007	23.5	2.6
China			
France	2006 – 2008	18.0	1.9
Germany			
India			
Indonesia			
Italy	2006 – 2008	26.3	1.7
Japan			
Mexico 1/	2006 – 2008	11.2	3.1
Russia			
Saudi Arabia			
South Africa	2007 – 2008 FY	13.7	3.5
South Korea	2006 – 2008	17.7	3.0
Turkey	2006 – 2008 FY	23.6	2.1
United Kingdom	2006 – 2008 FY	20.9	1.9
United States	2006 – 2007 FY	18.2	1.9
Unweighted Average		17.5	2.3

Source: IMF Staff estimates based on G-20 survey.
1/ Shares of nonoil CIT revenue and total nonoil tax revenue.

This makes it clear that for every country, but particularly for Italy, Turkey, Canada and the UK, the role and influence of the financial sectors on their economies and government policies is fundamental to the country and its economic and public sector health.

Without bank taxes, countries fail. But with bank failures, countries fail. And that is their Catch-22 and the reason why this is so hard to change.

Between domestic interests and focus, aligned with the radically different ways in which this crisis has impacted each G20 nation, it is unlikely that we shall ever see a simple agreement of policy reform now, or at the G20 meeting in Toronto in June.

The G20 party is over ... or is it? (2009)

So the G20 meeting is over and has an agreement to spend over $1 trillion through the IMF on nations that are worthy. The other key agreements include:

◆ A lockdown on the tax regimes of countries where people hide place their wealth. The age of bank 'secrecy' is over they say, although I'm not sure that Switzerland, the Caymans and other nations will appreciate that very much. Mind you, the OECD has just listed the tax havens they views as uncooperative, with Costa Rica, Malaysia (Labuan), the Philippines and Uruguay singled out as "jurisdictions that have not committed to the internationally agreed tax standard";

◆ A crackdown on light touch regulation and particularly on hedge funds, credit rating agencies and the operations of banks in the Over-the-Counter, or 'shadow' banking markets;

- ◆ The creation of a new Financial Stability Board, which will focus upon financial stability across all major economies; and
- ◆ Measures to address the issues in the banking system by preventing excessive leverage and forcing banks to have higher reserve policies so that we avoid being left under-capitalised in a downturn again.

There's a lot more to it, but I guess the key implications for banks are that there will be a fundamental rethinking of core products and services as:

- ◆ All systemically important financial institutions will be covered by the rules, including hedge funds;
- ◆ Capital requirements will change provisioning, and this may lead to a new Basel III;
- ◆ The current Financial Stability Forum becomes the Financial Stability Board and will embrace all G20 countries, the European Commission and Spain;
- ◆ The new Board will have a much wider mandate to promote financial stability, set financial guidelines and monitor supervisors for the major cross-border institutions; and
- ◆ Challenges in using cross-border tax loopholes for profits and products.

On the last one, I just realised something. One of my bank friends works in London two to three days a week, but lives in a tax haven called Monaco to escape tax here. Surely now, he'll move to Costa Rica. Nice weather, and no pressure from the G20 on his tax.

Maybe they should register the bank's head office there too?

Anyway, the G20 Summit was a useful step forward as it gathered clarity from the world's largest nations in stemming this crisis and moving forward. It was useful, even though all of the agreements were made beforehand by the civil servants.

76

The Road to London (2009)

The UK government has just published a document titled 'The Road to the London Summit'. This represents Gordon Brown's plan for getting the global economy back on track through a new global deal.

The report sets out the 'Global Deal' – a package of internationally co-ordinated measures to restore stability in the financial systems, and set a course for a sustainable recovery.

Actions include:

◆ Stimulate the global economy and help reduce the severity and length of the global recession for families and businesses in every country;

◆ Kick-start lending so businesses and families can borrow again and businesses have the resources to invest for the future;

◆ Renounce protectionism, with a transparent mechanism to monitor commitments and measures to increase access to trade finance;

◆ Reform international regulation to close regulatory gaps;

◆ Reform of the international financial institutions and the creation of an international early warning system, with a strengthened role for the IMF;

◆ Co-ordinated international action to build tomorrow today: to put the world economy on an economically, environmentally and socially sustainable path to recovery and growth, ensuring that these benefits extend to the poorest.

The document lays the basis for the G20 London Summit meeting on 2nd April 2009.

Meanwhile, according to Reuters, four working groups are preparing reports for the Summit. They will report to a meeting on March 14th of G20 finance ministers and central bank heads, and each group has two chairmen: one from an industrialised country and one from a developing country.

The groups are as follows:

1) Enhancing sound regulation and strengthening transparency.

Remit: Strengthen international standards in the areas of accounting, disclosure and risk, seek to provide greater consistency for regulatory regimes.

Co-chairs: Rakesh Mohan, Deputy Governor of the Reserve Bank of India, and Tiff Macklem, Associate Deputy Minister, Canadian Ministry of Finance

2) Reinforcing international cooperation and promoting integrity in financial markets.

Remit: Strengthen the management and resolution of cross-border financial crises, protect the global financial system from illicit activities.

Co-chairs: Alejandro Werner, Deputy Minister of Finance Mexican Ministry of Finance, and Joerg Asmussen, State Secretary in the German Federal Ministry of Finance

3) Reforming the International Monetary Fund (IMF)

Remit: Look at the role, governance and resource requirements of the IMF.

Co-chairs: Lesetja Kganyago, Director General of the South African National Treasury, and Mike Callaghan, Special Envoy International Economy (Australia)

4) The World Bank and other multilateral development banks

Remit: Consider the mandates, governance, resourcing and policy instruments of the MDBs in light of the needs of their members and the pressures resulting from the impact of the downturn on developing countries.

Co-chairs: Anggito Abimanyu, Head of Fiscal Policy at the Indonesian Ministry of Finance, and Benoit Coeure, Head of Multilateral Affairs and Development Policy at the French Ministry of Finance

Meanwhile, Gordon Brown has been rumoured to be taking on a role as head of the new Global Financial Regulator to sort out this mess, although he's denying that.

Chapter 3 Regulators' reaction

Introduction

Once the politicians have sorted out their act, the next group to rally to action are the regulators. Interestingly, the regulators that everyone looked towards for leadership – the Federal Reserve and Securities and Exchange Commission (SEC) in the USA, and the Financial Services Authority (FSA) and Bank of England in the UK – were the same regulators who were being lambasted by all for their failure to supervise. This has resulted in significant restructuring of bank supervision and yet, for all their failings, it was and is the regulators who have to make banks work. This is because the role of the regulator is to create rules and, more importantly, to enforce them. And some might say that it was the failure of enforcement rather than regulation that caused the issues we faced at the end of the last decade. Or maybe it was both ...

The future of banking regulation (2010)

The City of London released an interesting document yesterday on the future of regulation of banking. They talk about liquidity, leverage, capital and risk liberally, and state that the future regulatory regime must not clamp down on capital reserves in banking so hard that the banks are unable to lubricate the global economy.

What I found interesting is that there are quite a few contradictions in the 77-page report although, to be honest, I only read the Executive Summary.

From this summary, it's interesting that they plead that the macroprudential structures don't squeeze capital ratios, but hardly talk at all about the leverage issues Lehman Brothers created.

If my memory serves me, Lehman was operating at leverage ratios of up to 1:40, e.g. for every $1 of capital, $40 was being used to 'gamble' on the global markets. I also remember that their debts at bankruptcy were around $400 billion and BarCap estimated that for every $1 of debt, around $20 of CDS were being leveraged against Lehman's AAA rating. In other words, $8 trillion of leverage was in the system off the back of Lehman Brothers.

That was the issue, particularly when this leverage – and therefore liquidity – disappeared overnight.

Following on from this, they refer to the fact that the crisis was not caused by a lack of capital, but by a lack of liquidity. True, but I did not gather a clear view on liquidity risk or leverage ratios from the document. It may be in there, but it's hard to find.

For example, in Section Five that addresses leverage ratios, the report states that: "Judgement and discretion are vital, including judgement and discretion concerning circumstances under which firms will be permitted temporarily to have capital that is inadequate. The notion of employing a leverage ratio as a last-resort backstop to limit the damage caused by regulatory get-arounds arises precisely because of the limited ability and appetite of regulatory authorities for exercising discretion. That core problem is the one to address."

A bit of fudge there, if you ask me.

The same is true on liquidity risk, with the report proposing a global liquidity standard and yet they then say that they are "unconvinced that there is a case yet made for pursuing significant further deepening of international co-ordination of banking regulation. Indeed, we believe it quite likely that greater exercise of national discretion is the appropriate path forwards."

Now I understand the conundrum that you cannot have one nation regulate for example to stop bank bonuses as it will just mean bankers jump across to other nations. So you need a global agreement of some form. Equally, no global agreement will work, as there is always gold-plating and protectionism of national instruments, so you need a global framework with local interpretation.

That is kinda what they've proposed, but it's rather unclear. For example, their closing comment on liquidity is:

"In our view, improving liquidity standards are amongst the most important and material changes to be introduced – though they are likely to have high costs that must be recognised. However, the scope for international standards to deliver adequate liquidity is limited without increased roles for national lenders of last resort and in particular an increased role for central banks in prudential supervision."

In fact, the regular mantra in the document appears to be the frictions and tensions between global and local. For example, they state that there is a "risk that regulation will not apply evenly or that regulation will apply in the UK before the rest of the world", and that this "is seen as a significant threat to London's competitiveness. It is therefore widely urged that the Basel measures enact a common international timetable. International firms that operate in multiple markets are particularly keen to see common, consistent frameworks and standards applied."

Yet, as mentioned, they don't think regulation will or can be applied consistently across multiple markets.

All in all, more questions raised than answers in this document, but worth a read for those who are technically minded and interested.

Will regulators destroy the banking system? (2010)

On April 1st, the European Commission announced their key work plans for 2010. The plans are wide-ranging and imply a fundamental restructuring of the European banking markets.

If you don't think it's going that far, then think again, as a wide range of strategic initiatives were announced, including a new European supervision architecture and proposals in areas covering everything from derivatives markets, short selling and credit default swaps, deposit guarantee schemes, market abuse, crisis management tools and bank capital requirements. On this last point, they are even mooting a bank levy to generate €50 billion in case of future bailouts.

Alongside all of this, you have the hoo-ha of Paul Volcker's proposals on getting rid of bank prop trading, which has now been shot down, and Gordon Brown's Tobin tax which may go by-the-by as a result of the UK general election.

Whichever way you look at it though, we have governments and regulators everywhere saying that things must change, and trying to work out how to change things.

Then you have all of the committees, such as the UK's Treasury Select Committee and the US congressionally chartered Financial Crisis Inquiry Commission, who are bank bashing on regular occasion to try to work out what things to change.

In the case of the latter, they've had regular visitations from bank leaders and other besmirched economists and thinkers, to find out what caused the financial car crash of 2008.

Of note in this parade of failed financial acolytes was the appearance of Alan Greenspan, the highly esteemed and now generally blamed former head of the US Federal Reserve. Mr. Greenspan makes regular appearances, blaming the crisis on everything from the fall of the Berlin Wall and China's emergence through globalisation, to the banks leveraging of subprime and complex trade-off and packaging of such debt through complex financial instruments.

In fact, about the only accurate thing he has said recently is that: "Regulators who are required to forecast have had a woeful record of chronic failure. History tells us they cannot identify the

The Extraordinary Madness of Banks

timing of a crisis, or anticipate exactly where it will be located or how large the losses and spillovers will be ... nor can they fully eliminate the possibility of future crises."

Now I don't want to make this a Greenspan bashing column, as that would be too easy, but I do want to pick up on that phrase: "a woeful record", as it is very relevant to where we are today.

For example, as the European Commission considers its wide-ranging changes, I could pick up on many of their previous attempts to regulate the markets that have yet to succeed and would beg the question: why don't you fix what you started whilst starting to work out what to fix?

After all, we have Basel III, UCITS IV, Solvency II and CRD IV all coming up. Notice something about those? Yes, they are all updates of earlier regulations that did not work as expected.

We have the same with regulations such as MiFID, the Markets in Financial Instruments Directive. In the 2010 workplan, the European Commission announced that they were going to be taking a review of MiFID to make legislative proposals that would include the "dark pools issue". What this demonstrates is the law of unintended consequences, where MiFID has made everything electronified, fragmented and opaque. The opposite of some of its intentions, which were for transparency and a level playing field.

In summary, what worries me right now is: first, that the regulators and policymakers are scrabbling around not knowing what to do; second, that they have obviously got it wrong in the past; third, that they are woeful at working at the future; and finally, that their whole focus on shaking up the banking system will destroy it.

Not being too much of a scaremonger, am I?

Europe's new regulatory agenda (2010)

We had a fascinating and packed meeting at the Financial Services Club this week with David Doyle, EU Policy Advisor, discussing the challenges of the new Barosso European Parliament and their legislative drive in financial services.

David is a regular visitor to the Financial Services Club, and runs our European Financial Regulatory Advisory Group.

In a broad and wide ranging speech, he presented key views around MiFID, the PSD, Solvency II, UCITS IV, Basel III and more, as well as commentary on Jacques de Larosière's committee and the appointment of Michel Barnier to succeed Charlie McCreevy.

Here's a summary of the key points David made.

The Commission is taking a 'safety first approach' to regulating capital markets and market actors, and will fill in the gaps where European or national regulation is insufficient or incomplete.

The over-riding principles of their approach are that:

◆ All that is of systemic importance should be regulated and supervised;

◆ There is a need for a better well-capitalised finance industry, with less leverage;

◆ The Commission must legislate to avoid the perverse incentives in the financial sector that encourage excessive risk taking or over-reward;

◆ Supervision should have the right tools to grasp complex, inter-connected and globalised financial activities; and

◆ To restore trust, investors and consumers should benefit from clearer, more coherent and effective safeguards.

At this point, audience members asked lots of questions about whether the European approach would be the same as, or co-ordinated with, the US approach. David's feeling is that it is being co-ordinated on the big ticket items – risk, leverage, capital, bonuses and such like – but the rest is still open competition in terms of the way payments, capital markets and specific aspects of the market are operating, such as hedge funds.

There are then the key changes that should be introduced by the new Barosso team in the near term as a result of the de Larosière report. Of these changes, David believes that the new supervisory bodies will be key here. These are:

◆ European Securities and Markets Authority (ESMA);
◆ European Banking Authority (EBA) ;
◆ European Insurance and Occupational Pensions Authority (EIOPA).

These new authorities will have teeth, and will be responsible for ensuring that any EU member states who are not following the line of regulatory oversight are brought to order.

This will be in play within two years:

◆ 2009–2010: National FSAs powers strengthened, plus a focus on harmonising national rules to reduce cross-border differences ;
◆ 2011–2012: Implement EU-wide supervision via ESMA/EBA/EIOPA which will mean that the large states which are proactively interpreting directives will be in a far stronger position than those states resisting such supervision;

In practice, this means the UK and the Netherlands are going to be fine; France and Germany will have some wrinkles to iron out; other nations will get a note to say they need to fine-tune some stuff; and Spain and Italy will get a large wet fish slapped around their chops. After all, every Directive I deal with – MiFID and the PSD in particular – it's Spain and Italy which always seem to be dragging their heels.

David also made an interesting point here, which is that not only will the new regulatory bodies have teeth to drag member states before Brussels to explain why they are dragging their heels, but also resources to assist when assistance is needed. Therefore, in the case of Sweden where their key person for transposition of the PSD left at a critical juncture, this future structure would allow the EBA – the European Banking Authority which is not to be confused with the EBA, the Euro Banking Association that operates STEP2 and EURO1 – to provide people to fill the gaps. These people may be promoted in from regulatory authorities in other EU member states for example and, in so doing, it will fill the gaps.

A happy medium for macroprudential supervision (2009)

In the dialogue of the past week or so, an interesting theme has emerged. The theme is globally harmonised rules.

In fact, there appears to be a tectonic plate shift towards some form of global neutrality. What I mean by this is that historically, the English have disliked the French and vice versa; the Americans have been wary of the Russians and vice versa; and the Chinese have not trusted most nations, and most nations have not trusted the Chinese. I get a sense that this is changing.

With the last world war between nations a half a century ago, when we realised the loss of life was too intolerable to bear, we have had a tense but workable trading relationship worldwide ever since. That trading relationship has been brought to a head over the past year though, as the credit crisis strained all cross-border trade and finance relationships.

America and China were rumoured to be starting trade wars; Russia clamped down on dissident bloggers and media reporting; Europe split into pro-banking and anti-banking blocks; and everyone has been on tenterhooks to see how the world and,

The Extraordinary Madness of Banks

more specifically, the G20, would work out these issues. And there's the rub: the G20 has to work out these issues and act in unison. Unilateral actions from one country, such as taxing bankers' bonuses, will just result in banks and bankers moving to other financial centres to avoid the unilateral actions.

(...)

We appear to be moving away from free markets and principles-based regulation to tightly controlled markets with Napoleonic law. The problem with the Napoleonic approach is that it means everything has to be written into the rules. That is because if it's not in the rules, then it is assumed to be permissible. Hence, you end up with rule upon rule, and bureaucracy upon bureaucracy.

So there has to be a happy medium between free market disciplines with self-regulation and tightly monitored markets with strong regulators.

All in all, what the G20 movement seems to be moving towards therefore is global macroprudential supervisory structures that will strike a balance between leveraged collateral coverage, entrepreneurialism and individual innovation with appropriate market checks and balances, and free markets structures with tightly coupled regulations.

Although some of these drivers, structures, rules and procedures appear to be at opposites with each other, what it really means is that the G20 has to navigate towards a globally agreed approach that works for all.

Tough call but, if they can do it, a worthwhile goal to strive for.

The biggest danger is that we end up with rules that operate based upon the lowest common denominator. This is what we have ended up with in Europe, where all Directives are agreed to cater for the least sophisticated member state at the expense of the sophistication of the most developed states.

Or that's what people are telling me in the banks, as they are forced to obsolete highly functional systems for ones that are less functional as a result of EU directives.

This game of macroprudential supervisory structures will be an interesting one to observe, and to discover whether we get the best or worst of all worlds ... or, most likely, something in between.

What's next for the EU in light of the financial crisis? (2009)

Eurofi had their annual conference in Gothenburg, Sweden last month. The meeting was themed 'What are the priorities for the incoming EU authorities in the light of the financial crisis' and saw a number of common themes recur in discussions by key policymakers, officials and industry figures.

Here is their summary of the meeting.

While it is clear that the worst of the crisis is behind us, we are not out of the woods yet.

This is in large part because one of the main underlying contributors to the crisis has not gone away: the existence of moral hazard. Indeed, it has probably got worse in the financial system because of the implicit acknowledgement that some institutions are too big or to interconnect to fail has in many cases become explicit.

This is an issue not just for the financial authorities but also for the single market. A total of €3 trillion has been injected into the EU's financial sector, but it has been distributed unevenly, creating potential distortions of the competitive landscape.

For this reason, as well as the massive burden placed on public finances, it is important to start thinking about an exit strategy that can extricate governments from some of Europe's largest financial groups.

The Extraordinary Madness of Banks

However, the financial sector faces enormous issues of trust – the public has been appalled by what's happened. Many market participants have lost faith in each other, partly because the value of so many impaired assets remains so uncertain.

The debate continues over whether banks will be forced to narrow their activities, with influential figures such as Paul Volcker, economic adviser to President Obama, speaking out in favour of restrictions, while many in the industry argue that it was not business models that were to blame for the crisis but poor execution.

There is clear consensus that the crisis revealed unsuspected systemic risks and that these must be dealt with. Self-regulation has been thoroughly discredited and new regulation is on the way or has already been introduced in an attempt to harness the momentum for change that much fear is running out as the crisis recedes.

It is agreed that regulation and supervision of individual financial entities is not enough – there must be oversight of macro systemic risks as well, and this oversight must be linked to micro-prudential regulation, not just in the EU but on a global basis.

The industry is clearly unhappy at the weight of new regulation. Jacques de Larosière warns that there are dangers of unintended consequences from the overlapping of the various initiatives. Moreover, a system of ratios that would be to some extent disconnected from effective risks would do nothing to address the causes of this crisis. These measures will have a disproportionate impact on Europe where bank intermediation is far more developed than in the US.

However, policymakers have become more confident in their assertions that there are restrictions to the sector's freedom that are justified for the good of the system as a whole.

Nonetheless, it is recognised that significant challenges remain in implementing the regulation.

An unprecedented level of communication and co-operation will be necessary to ensure that overkill and regulatory arbitrage are avoided.

There must also be a re-examination of the financial system, of its role and size, some participants said. The world faces a range of significant, long-term challenges such as climate change, scarcity of natural resources and ageing population. Dealing with these requires a more long-term outlook from investors that has been lacking in recent years and to tackle obstacles long-term investment has to face up.

The regulatory framework of OTC derivatives and alternative investment funds (AIFs) is also being reviewed with the objective to bring additional safety to the financial system. The industry, however, points out that constraints that may be unnecessary from a risk mitigation perspective. Constraints potentially damaging to customer needs should be avoided, and the specificities of the products concerned should be well taken into account. The risk management processes of management companies should also be revised in light of the financial crisis and the responsibilities and liabilities of the players operating along the fund value chain should also be clarified.

Finally, the ongoing actions to improve the efficiency and competitiveness of cash equity infrastructures (MiFID and the Code of Conduct) should not create new risks particularly when implementing interoperability between CCPs.

As Jean-Claude Trichet, President of the European Central Bank, said: "While a lot has been achieved, a lot remains to be done."

The Extraordinary Madness of Banks

Stress tests useful or misleading? (2010)

Having spent much of the weekend absorbing the European bank stress test results, I've got to ask why they bothered.

OK, so it was to get bank share prices up, but the whole thing was just a typical European sham where every country does things in a different way, with the whole thing designed to cover up the real weaknesses in the European banking system.

Bearing in mind that the stress tests were called to shore up confidence in the system due to the concerns in the markets over a sovereign default in Greece or Spain, the fact that the tests left out that particular scenario is ridiculous.

In case you didn't catch it, the tests looked at a double dip recession and a sovereign debt shock, but purely based upon debt that banks were trading, not debt that banks had in their vaults.

Now I blogged a while back about the fact that Europe's banks held over $1 trillion in debt to just Greece and Spain.

With sovereign debt trading on the bank's books worth about a tenth of their total exposure, that means that around $900 billion of potential sovereign debt has been ignored. How this can be ignored is beyond me.

Secondly, the tests ignore any liquidity risk issues, and just looked at market and credit risks. Why?

This crisis started with liquidity risk when interbank lending dried up, and then exploded when sovereign debt became a major concern. The fact that CEBS left out these two clearly important dimensions just seems silly.

But then it is purely a politically motivated exercise to try to stop the haemorrhaging of confidence in the European system.

Now, I actually went to the press briefing on Friday night – a time chosen to ensure that markets could not react immediately to this sham – and saw the baying hounds of the media looking totally incredulous as the headlines were announced.

"We have seven bank failures that, between them, in the most adverse scenario would need €3.5 billion of new capital."

I'm sorry, but that's nuts.

When the Americans did their stress tests, half their banks failed and they needed $75 billion of new capital. So how come, in the worst of situations, our banks would only need €3.5 billion and fewer than 10% fail?

Because it's a fix. It's fixed because each country interpreted the stress test conditions for unemployment and house prices and other economic conditions in their own way.

It's fixed because each regulator and central bank applied the test conditions against their bank's balance sheets in different ways.

And it's fixed by leaving out the sovereign debt exposures and potential defaults on the bank's books.

Nevertheless, something useful did come out of it: data. There's lots of data about the state of the bank's balance sheets released by CEBS that can now be analysed by the markets, rather than the fudge that the regulators applied. Therefore, with the reservations stated above, I went through the numbers over the weekend and found an interesting result.

First, a little explanation of the numbers.

The tests are based upon three scenarios.

Scenario 1 is the benchmark, which is based upon the current ECB forecasts for macroeconomic developments across the European Union.

Scenario 2 is then based upon a double dip recession, which sees no growth in 2010 and a 0.4% downturn in GDP in the European Union in 2011, versus 1% in 2010 and 1.7% forecasted in the benchmark.

The Extraordinary Madness of Banks

Scenario 3 studies the impact of a sovereign debt shock to the European Union on top of this recession, and is geared towards higher debt losses and impairments in the PIIGS – Portugal, Ireland, Italy, Greece and Spain – than in other countries.

This does not assume a sovereign default, just corporate debt and sovereign debt on the trading books of the banks. That's about 10% of the total exposure for the banks, should a country default.

In the CEBS tests, they looked at Tier 1 capital ratio – not core capital, just Tier 1 capital – and said that the ratio should not fall under 6%. Under the EU Capital Requirements Directive, as it stands uncorrected since this crisis hit, the lowest level by law is 4%. Meanwhile, the likelihood is that a minimum 8% Tier 1 capital will be required in the future and, in this context, is a far better ratio to apply.

For example, based upon the CEBS view of the world, using the combined worst case of a double dip recession and a sovereign debt shock, they find seven banks would fall under the 6% Tier 1 capital ratio level: five in Spain, one in Germany and one in Greece.

Looking at the numbers using an 8% Tier 1 capital levels – a level that is rumoured to be required under revised terms for EU bank trading in the future – 39 banks would fail in the worst-case scenario: one in Austria, one in Cyprus, five in Germany, three in Greece, two in Ireland, four in Italy, one in Portugal, one in Slovenia and 21 in Spain.

That would have been a far more realistic number to have announced and, based upon the fragmented application and interpretation of the tests by member states, is probably more likely to be the worst-case scenario than the seven bank failures CEBS announced last Friday.

Note: Failure does not means the banks are insolvent just undercapitalised, and so this would have been a much better way for CEBS, the ECB and the European Commission to have achieved some credibility from this exercise.

Stressed? Don't worry. The French and Germans will sort it out ... (2010)

The reason CEBS, the European Commission and European Central Bank gave for not including the scenario of a sovereign default in the stress tests is that they just don't think it's going to happen.

"It is not possible", they said. "Why", we asked. "Because it is just incredibly unlikely and, even if anything did start to fragment in the fissures of finance in Greece or Spain, we have the European Financial Stability Fund (EFSF) to solve it", they replied.

Now that's an interesting statement ... because it is also a fuddle. The EFSF is a €440 billion fund designed to cover any sovereign debt crisis in Europe in the future. Therefore, the concept of a bank being exposed to huge losses from Greece and Spain is no longer an issue. That is the logic. And it's quite good. But it's already been shot to pieces.

Ken Wattret, a market analyst with BNP Paribas, performed a really interesting analysis of the EFSF and issued a note in July that provides a clear Q&A overview. Here's my summary of Ken's research note:

> The EFSF is a limited liability company based in Luxembourg announced in May as a measure to "preserve financial stability in Europe". Its CEO is Klaus Regling, a former senior German Finance Ministry official who worked on the preparations for EMU and who has also worked at the IMF.

> The purpose of the EFSF, according to its terms of reference, is "to collect funds and provide loans in conjunction with the

IMF to cover the financing needs of Eurozone member states in difficulty, subject to strict conditionality".

According to the Framework Agreement, the EFSF will finance the provision of loans via the issuance of "bonds, notes, commercial paper, debt securities or other financing arrangements" which will be backed by unconditional and irrevocable guarantees from those member states which participate.

Only the member states of the Eurozone participate in the scheme, providing guarantees up to a total of €440bn on a pro-rata basis.

If a Eurozone member state seeks assistance from the EFSF, they must initially agree a Memorandum of Understanding (MoU) with the European Commission, in liaison with the IMF and the ECB. This MoU will set out the budgetary and economic policy conditions which the Eurozone member state must comply with in order to receive financial assistance.

The detailed terms and conditions would then be set out in a Loan Facility Agreement which is subject to the agreement of all the guarantors (i.e. those countries in the EFSF).

The EFSF will enter into force when five or more member states, comprising at least two-thirds of the total guarantees, have confirmed that they have concluded the necessary procedures under their national legislation. It will last for almost three years, with the guarantees applying to loans made on or before 30 June 2013.

Now then, what Mr. Wattret did next is the most intriguing part. He produced a chart which shows that Germany and France contribute almost half of all of the ECB's capital for this scheme, whilst the PIIGS – Portugal, Italy, Ireland, Greece and Spain –

contribute almost 35% of the scheme, with Italy and Spain representing 30%. Greece does not contribute anything to the scheme at this time for obvious reasons.

So what the ECB is saying is that the $1 trillion exposure of European banks to the sovereign debt of just Greece and Spain, as discussed yesterday, can be covered by the €440 billion available in an emergency through this scheme.

But let's take this a step further. Say Spain gets into distress and has to leave the scheme. That removes a further 12% of the scheme's funding. In fact, should Spain have issues, the burden on France and Germany increases by a further 7% of the fund – or an additional €7.5 billion to bring their number to a total of €250 billion between them.

This is what prompted me to ask at the end of the CEBS press conference: "So what you're really saying is that you didn't use the scenario of a sovereign default because you believe French and German citizens will be happy to bail out Spain like they did with Greece?"

That didn't go down well but it had to be asked and, no matter how unlikely it is for this to occur, it is the reality of the situation.

John McFall and the return of Glass-Steagall (2010)

John McFall kindly agreed to explain a bit about the work of the Treasury Select Committee to the Financial Services Club.

Here's what he said (loosely written, so none of this should be taken as direct quotation).

The UK Treasury Select Committee is a Governmental Select Committee established to look at the future of banking in 1989. It has particularly made progress since 1997, when the Bank of England was separated from the Treasury, as it is now playing a

The Extraordinary Madness of Banks

key role in scrutinising the activities of the Treasury, the Bank and the FSA.

We have been sitting near enough in permanent session since the collapse of Northern Rock in August 2007, and ours has been the only body to sit as a direct interaction between Parliament and the public in terms of how we are able to communicate the issues to the people.

For example, we had the Chancellor of the Exchequer, the Governor of the Bank of England and the Head of the FSA appearing together before the committee recently and our website received over 6,000 questions from the general public just for that one meeting. This shows that they are so interested in this issue, and we give them a voice to talk to the tripartite authorities that run the financial system.

We focus upon financial stability and have established new financial stability procedures. There are two issues here that we are particularly concerned with.

First, the excessive attitude towards risk that we have seen over the past decade, as epitomised by HBOS and particularly the lending practices of the Bank of Scotland; and the lack of corporate governance in the sector, as shown specifically by the Royal Bank of Scotland's Fred Goodwin. This resulted in the new Banking Bill as announced in the Queen's speech last month, which will give the FSA stronger powers and as this is meant to be 'more intrusive regulation'.

Another big issue is what we call 'regulatory badging', where a company can stand back from their operations and duties of governance by saying that, if it gets into a mess, that it is the fault of the FSA. This is why the area of corporate governance still needs addressing further.

With regards to the future, in the New Year we are going to be looking at the potential for 'narrow banking'. Last year, this fell off the agenda when Lord Turner (the Chairman of the FSA) gave his report, but we want to bring this discussion back. The focus of the narrow banking review will be to find the answer to the question of how to avoid the public taxpayer having to pick up the tab if the financial markets go wrong. In other words, whether we need to be bring back the Glass-Steagall divide or not.

Mervyn King, the Governor of the Bank of England, has lobbied for the return of the Glass-Steagall Act – the post-Depression legislation in the USA that separated investment and retail banking, repealed in 1999 by the Gramm-Leach Bliley Act.

This way we could let an investment bank fail whilst the remainder – the payments processing, retail and commercial parts of the bank which must not fail – could be protected.

(...)

FSF proposals for strengthening the financial system (2009)

The Financial Stability Forum published their principles on strengthening the financial system yesterday. Here are the headlines.

Recommendations and principles to strengthen financial systems

On 2 April 2009, the Financial Stability Forum (FSF) issued reports covering:

- ◆ Recommendations for Addressing Procyclicality in the Financial System;
- ◆ Principles for Cross-border Cooperation on Crisis Management; and
- ◆ Principles for Sound Compensation Practices;

The Forum also published an update on the implementation of the recommendations contained in the FSF's April 2008 Report on Enhancing Market and Institutional Resilience.

Addressing procyclicality in the financial system

The present crisis has demonstrated the disruptive effects of procyclicality – mutually reinforcing interactions between the financial and real sectors of the economy that tend to amplify business cycle fluctuations and cause or exacerbate financial instability. Addressing procyclicality in the financial system is an essential component of strengthening the macroprudential orientation of regulatory and supervisory frameworks.

The recommendations set out in this report mitigate mechanisms that amplify procyclicality in both good and bad times. They encompass a mix of quantitative/rules-based and discretionary measures that are interrelated and reinforce one another. They will be implemented over time once conditions in financial markets return to normal.

Principles for cross-border co-operation on crisis management

Through these Principles, relevant authorities, including supervisory agencies, central banks and finance ministries, commit to co-operate both in making advanced preparations for dealing with financial crisis and in managing them.

Update on the Implementation of the April 2008 FSF Recommendations

The update on progress in implementing the recommendations of the April 2008 Report on Enhancing Market and Institutional Resilience covers actions in five areas:

(i) Strengthening capital, liquidity and risk management in the financial system;

(ii) Enhancing transparency and valuation;

(iii) Changing the role and uses of credit ratings;

(iv) Strengthening the authorities' responsiveness to risks; and

(v) Putting in place robust arrangements for dealing with stress in the financial system.

Principles for sound compensation practices

The Principles require compensation practices in the financial industry to align employees' incentives with the long-term profitability of the firm. The principles call for the following key principles to be implemented:

Effective governance of compensation

◆ The firm's board of directors must actively oversee the compensation system's design and operation;

◆ The firm's board of directors must monitor and review the compensation system to ensure the system operates as intended;

◆ Staff engaged in financial and risk control must be independent, have apppropriate authority, and be compensated in a manner that is independent of the business areas they oversee and commensurate with their key role in the firm.

Effective alignment of compensation with prudent risk taking

◆ Compensation must be adjusted for all types of risk;

◆ Compensation outcomes must be symmetric with risk outcomes;

◆ Compensation payout schedules must be sensitive to the time horizon of risks;

◆ The mix of cash, equity and other forms of compensation must be consistent with risk alignment.

Effective supervisory oversight and engagement by stakeholders

◆ Supervisory review of compensation practices must be rigorous and sustained, and deficiencies must be addressed promptly with supervisory action;

◆ Firms must disclose clear, comprehensive and timely information about their compensation practices to facilitate constructive engagement by all stakeholders.

The Extraordinary Madness of Banks

The report's opening lines say: "In the future, all the stake-holders of financial firms, including supervisors [or regulators], shareholders, and (where firms are systematically important) governments, will expect to receive more information about compensation policies and to increase their engagement with them."

The Financial Instability Report (2008)

The Bank of England released its Financial Stability Report today ... or should we rename this the Financial Instability Report, as that's what we've seen for the last few months.

The Report reviews the UK banking system every six months and started back in 1996. In that first report, the Bank said: "The most recent figures suggest that the banks are in good shape. They are strongly capitalised and, on that basis, well placed to expand their lending."

And that's just what they did. For example, today's report notes that UK banks had an equal amount of deposits to loans back in 2001 but, by 2007, had lent £700 billion more than they had on deposit.

£700 billion more than they had in deposits? Were they mad?

Yep, and that's why today's report opens with: "In recent weeks, the global financial system has undergone a period of exceptional instability. This instability was rooted in weaknesses within the financial system that developed during an extended global credit boom: rapid balance sheet expansion; the creation of assets whose liquidity and credit quality were uncertain in less benign conditions; and fragilities in funding structures. Whilst these weaknesses had been identified, including by the Bank in previous reports, few predicted they would lead to such disloca-tion in the global financial system."

Too darned right.

In fact, this report is very similar to the International Monetary Fund's Financial Stability Report:

> "With financial markets worldwide facing growing turmoil, internationally coherent and decisive policy measures will be required to restore confidence in the global financial system. Failure to do so could usher in a period in which the ongoing deleveraging process becomes increasingly disorderly and costly for the real economy. In any case, the process of restoring an orderly system will be challenging, as a significant deleveraging is both necessary and inevitable."

Similarly, the Financial Stability Forum released their recommendations earlier this month, which can be summarised as:

- Strengthened prudential oversight of capital, liquidity and risk management;
- Enhancing transparency and valuation;
- Changes in the role and uses of credit ratings;
- Strengthening the authorities' responsiveness to risks;
- Robust arrangements for dealing with stress in the financial system.

Now I'm not going to cast any aspersions on these laudable efforts, but you have to ask with so many regulatory authorities around, how come no-one spotted this before?

Sure, we can all rationalise it today in hindsight but, as Nassim Taleb pointed out on BBC's Newsnight, no-one forecast this crisis to be as severe as it's become.

In fact, what is common to all of these reports is that they all knew there were systemic risks in the markets, an overexpansion of lending and leveraged debt, inherent risks between economies and off-balance sheet issues … just that no-one forecast all this stuff would hit the fan at the same time. For example, the July 2006 Financial Stability Report from the Bank highlighted six areas of vulnerability under three key headings:

The Extraordinary Madness of Banks

Vulnerabilities in international financial markets

◆ If insurance premiums paid for carrying risks rose abruptly, asset prices would fall sharply;

◆ Financial imbalances among the major economies may unwind in a disorderly manner which would create significant credit and market risks.

Extended non-financial sector balance sheets

◆ Rapid releveraging of corporate loans against a background of underpriced corporate credit risk, could widen and deepen over time;

◆ There are signs of stress among a minority of households in terms of debt to income, with personal insolvencies rising sharply.

Structural dependencies within the financial system

◆ Large complex financial institutions balance sheets and risk-taking activities appear to be expanding and this could create systemic risks;

◆ Clearing and settling infrastructures may be inadequately understood and tested in the event of any disruption.

Of these six vulnerabilities, the first five all happened at once, and it was this threat that no-one foresaw. The threat they would all happen at once. Now it's obvious, because we can see that they are all inter-related, but before everyone thought "nah, they could never all happen at once".

What is the Bank recommending as a result?

Basically that leverage ratios are peeled back to manageable levels and that, over the medium term, a fundamental rethink of safeguards against systemic risk is needed. This rethink will include the development of new countercyclical tools and stronger capital and liquidity regulation.

In other words, banks need to set aside more money in the good times to cover the bad times. If there is a next time, the capital requirements will dictate that banks strengthen capital bases and increase liquidity through all the good years, with the size of reserves increasing based upon the levels of profitability.

The former head of the Financial Services Authority, Howard Davies, expanded upon this theme in an interesting article last week on how he would fix things. Mr. Davies has five recommendations:

- Simpler supervision with coverage across all sectors: banking, securities and insurance;
- Global inclusion to gain legitimacy as, right now, the Financial Stability Forum (FSF) "includes the Netherlands and Australia but not China or India";
- Faster operation, as you can't take another 10 years to create a Basel III ;
- Improving macro-economic management through the IMF and BIS, so that they can enforce increased levels of capital retention by banks through the boom times;
- Give the FSF more power by renaming it the Financial Stability Council, with powers designated by the G7 Finance Ministers to actually do something.

I particularly took note of the line he slipped into the article that reads: "when I became chairman of the United Kingdom's Financial Services Authority in 1997, the authority – Britain's only financial regulator – was a member of about 75 international bodies or committees. By the time I left in 2003, that number had doubled."

In other words, we had too many unco-ordinated regulators and policymakers, and this will change now.

So easy in hindsight, isn't it?

Can regulators really make markets more stable? (2008)

I found myself sceptically smiling when reading that the Financial Stability Forum is going to make the banking world safer by:

◆ Strengthening prudential oversight of capital, liquidity and risk management;
◆ Enhancing transparency and valuation;
◆ Changing the role and uses of credit ratings;
◆ Strengthening the authorities' responsiveness to risks; and
◆ Ensuring there are robust arrangements for dealing with stress in the financial system.

The reason why this hit me today is that the *Financial Times* reports that regulators, central banks and other supervisory authorities are now taking this report to create rules and regulations that will "make it far more expensive" for investment banks to use complex financial products, for example mortgage-backed securities, by taking away some of the VAR (Value-at-Risk) and 'warehousing' activities that led to the subprime crisis.

VAR rules allowed banks to keep just a small proportion of the capital reserves to cover the exposures of assets classed as low-risk, such as AAA-rated Structured Investment Vehicles. Equally, warehousing allowed investment banks to shore up various assets and then repackage and sell them off later. All of this created off-balance sheet activities that hid the real risk exposure of certain banks, and the combination of the use of VAR, warehousing and complex financial instruments, such as Collateralised Debt Obligations and Structured Investment Vehicles, led to the huge melt-down and write-offs of the UBS's and Citibank's of this world.

So why was I smiling sceptically?

Because the Financial Stability Forum was created in 1999 and, after almost a decade in operation, we have massive financial instability. But that's ok. You can correct these things, which is what they're doing, so that instability caused by this issue never occurs again.

Because the FSF "brings together senior representatives of national financial authorities (e.g. central banks, supervisory authorities and treasury departments), international financial institutions, international regulatory and supervisory groupings, committees of central bank experts and the European Central Bank." Well, we all know that they made a pig's ear of the last few years in supervising the markets, but that's ok, they'll fix the mess this time by tightening up rules and regulations to reflect the issues they are aware of.

Because, if the FSF and others could be effective, then why do the markets collapse every few years and why did one investment banker make the comment: "Chris, we work in cycles. Our cycle is four years – expect three good years with bonuses, and one bad one." In other words, every fourth year, the markets will suffer a blip. We just hope it is not a big blip and, if it is, that the authorities will bail us out (note: Bear Stearns, Northern Rock).

Because of a comment that rings in my ears ten years after reading the book Liar's Poker, where Salomon's General Counsel is talking about how they work and his comment is "My role is to find the chinks in the regulator's armour". In other words, to buck the markets and make real money, you have to find higher risk opportunities. Higher risks create higher returns. However, anything that has higher risk is generally frowned upon by regulators because it can cause markets to collapse. Therefore, they regulate it and investment banks, as a result, continually seek to find ways to break the regulations legally, in order to maximise liquidity, returns, alpha and all that good stuff.

Because all of these books are coming out at the moment, saying that regulators create market risks, rather than minimise them, as demonstrated above. In fact, certain regulatory folks, like Howard Davies, the former head of the FSA, are now saying financial market regulations must be global and consistent, not national or internationally inconsistent. Wow, there's a blinder of a statement in itself.

I could go on (and on and on and ...), but whatever the FSF and others implement, there will be flaws that allow bankers to find somewhere else in the market to find and make some real money.

Oh yes, as a sceptic, what is the answer therefore?

If the FSF's plans cannot work, where are the flaws?

The flaws are three-fold:

1. Regulating in hindsight after the horse has bolted;
2. Regulating locally rather than globally; and
3. Regulating in a vacuum.

Many times, we have all said that if you see a market boom, there will be a bust. So regulators should really be building scenario plans way in advance, as they see markets trending towards risk exposures that have uncalculated impacts.

Calculate those impacts.

The fact that Northern Rock went bust because their risk models purely calculated risks of a house price bubble bursting, rather than liquidity drying up, shows that their risk models were flawed. What we really need is regulators who have really good risk managers creating scenarios and working closely with markets to stress test the business assumptions and ideas that lie behind their product views. And then make those risk models the best they can possibly be.

I'm not saying that risk managers and scenario modelling are the answer alone. You need to apply these measures globally and consistently, which is one of the biggest challenges, but most of the regulators and central bankers I meet have little experience of today's cut and thrust trading floor. Very few have been in that environment, building risk models and trading with the front desk warriors in the real world. And, if they have, it is often a decade or more since they had that experience.

So … it's not the answer but, if regulators really want to plug the holes in their Swiss cheese legal structures, then hire a red-hot team of trading and risk folks from the real world who can test their regulatory armour for chinks before the market does. And then make sure you can apply your rules globally.

Seems like we still have a bumpy ride ahead.

Chapter 4 Banks' inaction?

Introduction

Whilst politicians and regulators run around trying to create new rules and policies, banks have also been active. Their actions were primarily directed at ensuring the new procedures and regulations would continue to work to their advantage, rather than tightening the noose so much that innovations in banking activities would become impossible. Whilst the policymakers were trying hard to return banks to their roots of lending when appropriate and investing where necessary, banks were trying hard to ensure that the high wave of profits made available through innovative investment markets would continue. The result has been a tension between willingness to change and support an agenda to avoid future crisis and a need to maintain the status quo to ensure that profitability and arbitrage could still be played as before. Some view this as banks' inaction, whilst others view it as the fine line between winners and losers. You make your own mind up.

Rethinking the customer experience (2010)

Just got a really interesting survey from Deloitte looking at the future of financial services. The document is based upon a survey of 200 industry execs, and garners their views across a broad brush of areas.

Interestingly, 89% of those surveyed believe their firm survived the crisis as expected or better than expected. I expect you can guess who's in the 11% who thought their firm suffered badly. Now most of them are looking at recovery and 88% are positive about the future ... I expect you can guess who's in the 12% who aren't.

Anyways, there are loads of question in there, but here's a few charts that really intrigued me.

In answer to the question: 'What strategic objectives of your business do you think have experienced the most long-term damage from the financial crisis and economic downturn?' more bankers than securities folks were worried about their ability to continue operating as they did in the past.

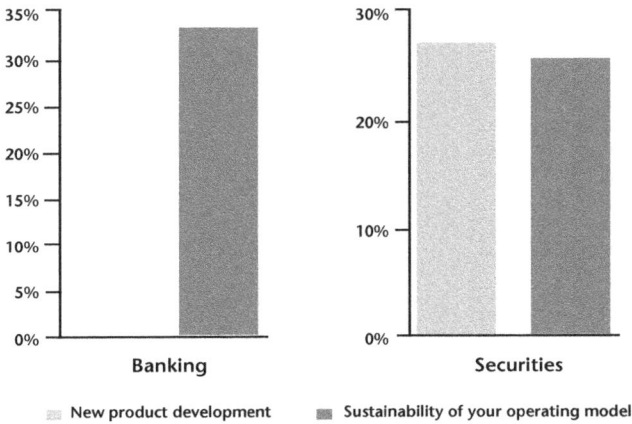

In fact, it amazes me that 66% of bankers and 75% of securities personnel are therefore answering this question as 'business as usual'. What planet are they on?

Similarly, when asked 'what positive opportunities have resulted from the financial crisis and economic downturn?', the answer is overwhelmingly that competitors have been squeezed out of the market but, more intriguingly, Europeans are far more focused upon cost reductions than the Americans.

Now, I keep hearing that this crisis was caused by US investment banks ... so how come it's Europe that's cutting the costs?

And what are they going to do strategically about it? Well, most are going to focus upon better measurement of risks.

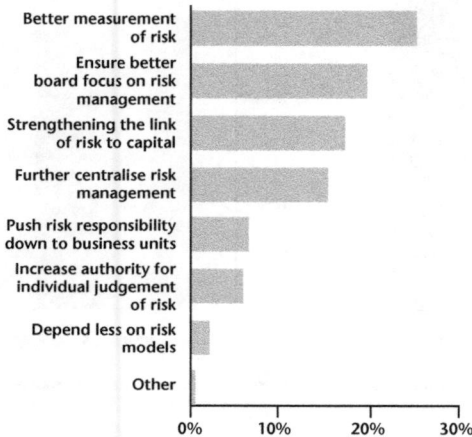

No wonder we all hear stuff about liquidity risk and real-time risk management these days.

Finally, most of the banks agree that it is customers and their relationship with customers that has been hit hardest by this crisis. Therefore their #1 focus is to rebuild relationships. How will they do that? By focusing upon improving the customer experience.

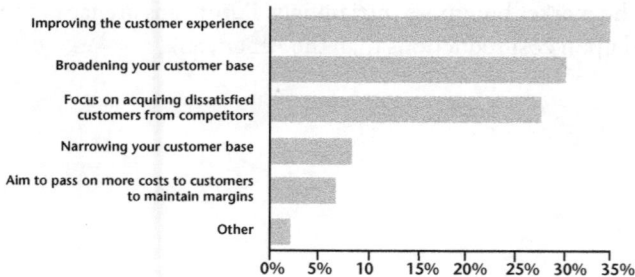

4 : Banks' inaction?

Now then, who's doing that? What examples are out there of customer experience improvements? Aha, I know one. Checkout BBVA's ATM of the Future.

Fascinating stuff.

The land of a thousand voices (2010)

It seems that I'm having a long whinge and rant all week, but I'm trying not to.

What I'm really trying to do is to get some answers to this crisis of confidence in the banks and, consequently, the banking system. This is nothing to do with the credit crisis, but the response of the banks to the credit crisis, which is to trash all trust and confidence in their ethics and approach.

This is why there is this non-stop bleating about bonuses and interest rates. The banks justify this behaviour on the basis of all the other kids on the block are doing it so, if we didn't, we would just get beaten up in the banking playground by the bonus bullies. Stephen Hester of RBS said today that: "employees are leaving because it was offering lower bonuses than City rivals". He also said that profits at the bank, which is 84 per cent owned by the taxpayer, would have been about £1 billion higher if it had managed to stop staff leaving. The bank said it had "paid the minimum necessary to retain and motivate staff who are critical to the recovery of RBS".

Trouble is, this doesn't cut the mustard. MPs warned that the public would be astonished that the bank was paying £1.3 billion in bonuses, given that it today reported a £3.6 billion loss for last year.

But none of these arguments raging in the media address the real issue here. The real issue is not bonuses, profits, lending or

The Extraordinary Madness of Banks

interest rates. The real issue is a lack of internal market leadership within the banking industry.

Nothing to do with regulators, politicians or press. The most significant failure has been the inability for the industry to act as a cohesive whole to respond to the issues arising under their watch.

Instead we act as a fragmented group of a thousand voices. Individual voices stand up and are counted, and some count more than others such as the Jamie Dimons, John Varleys and Stephen Greens. But nothing is co-ordinated or arranged in a way that makes sense or alleviates the public anger and distrust in the system.

Take the example of the past week of bankers' bonuses. Initially, one bank – Barclays – set an example of waiving bonuses payments, as their leaders chose to repeat the actions of a year earlier and declined the multimillion pound pot they were entitled to. Reluctantly, the rest then followed with RBS, Lloyds and now HSBC one-by-one agreeing not to award their leader's bonus.

The result is that they were accused of being lame sheep in doing so, just following the lead of one, and it just looked limp. It also rang of insincerity anyway, in that several of these leaders are purely deferring bonuses and have taken large swags of cash via other means (e.g. Bob Diamond's $46 million payout on the sale of Barclays Global Investors last year) or just don't need it as most are on million-pound plus packages. In fact, one cynic said that there would just be a top-up of their pension pots to compensate, and so no-one sees these token gestures as being anything other than that – token.

Does this justify the payouts to their investment banking teams by making such sacrifices? No. Does it restore faith and trust and displace the anger and mistrust?

No. So all it's done is served as some form of internal justification for the continuance of mega-bonus payments to investment banking staff.

The issue still lies with the press, politicians and regulators, however: in this land of 1,000 voices, where no one co-ordinated single voice resonates, where is the leadership to change the system?

Take the example I've just given. What bankers should have done is worked together to create a co-ordinated plan across the sector pre-emptively and early on. For example, Stephen Hester (RBS), John Varley and Bob Diamond (Barclays), Eric Daniels (Lloyds) and Michael Geoghegan (HSBC) see each other often enough in front of Treasury Select Committees to be able to co-ordinate their responses. So why didn't they all agree upfront to defer leaders' bonus payments, and announce this as a co-ordinated approach pre-results season? A joint announcement of rationale and reasoning would have been far more powerful than the sheep mentality manner of following the leader.

Equally, Jamie 'Demon' Dimon (JPMC), Vikram Pandit (Citi), Lloyd Blankfein (Goldman Sachs), Brian Moynihan (Bank of America) and John Mack (Morgan Stanley) see each other all the time in front of Federal Committees. So why didn't these leaders co-ordinate responses to bailouts and bonuses?

You may say they did, but not from an observer's viewpoint externally. It looks like maverick individual actions and approaches, with no single voice to rally the industry to a resolution.

Why these 'leaders' cannot organise themselves is beyond comprehension. After all, if these global CEOs of banks had created a co-ordinated and rational campaign to cap bonuses, waive their own, provide charitable donations, show how bank lending and bailouts had been atoned, then the media, public and politicians would not be baying for their blood.

The fact that: (a) there is no single voice of leadership that is co-ordinated across these banks speaking on their behalf; and (b) these leaders have allowed banks to behave without change, as

The Extraordinary Madness of Banks

they were before and as if nothing had happened, is going to lead to a showdown.

That showdown is not far away and, according got all my sources, will be far more draconian and vicious than any action that would have been taken if the industry had spoken with one voice, rather than a thousand.

But then, this industry's ability to self-regulate with transparency and integrity historically has been pretty poor so this comes as little surprise.

Banking on the banking system, one year later (2009)

At a recent event, the plenary session was all about 'leading through uncertainty' with:

- ◆ Peter Sands, Group Chief Executive of Standard Chartered;
- ◆ Ronnie Chan, Chairman of Hang Lung Properties Ltd; and
- ◆ Bill White, Chair of the OECD Economic and Development Review Committee,

discussing the state of the banking industry one year after its near-destruction and chaired by Martin Wolf, Chief Economics Commentator for the *Financial Times*.

Here's my summary of how their conversation went:

Martin Wolf: Is the financial system healed?

Peter Sands: 'Healed' is too strong a word. Better yes, but healed is too strong. For me, think of the patient as dying and now we've moved out of the operating theatre and intensive care, but that doesn't mean the financial system has left the hospital.

We still have huge imbalances which are an issue for the world economy and financial system and we still need to take leverage out of the system which has begun, but not happened to any-where near the level it needs to yet.

Governments and central banks have thrown huge amounts of money at the system as well, but without an exit strategy.

Then there are a whole slew of things for the regulatory architecture to fix and, finally, there's a lot that we as banks need to mend as the business models of some of the banks are just not sustainable. For example, one of the biggest banking models until this time last year was the US broker-dealer model. Within a week of Lehman Brothers collapsing, that model ceased to exist, and the ramifications of that demise are still to filter through in terms of the wholesale lending markets.

At present, those markets have the support of the funding from central banks but, when that goes, then there will be further questions. For example, the cost of credit will go up and policymakers seem to think that banks and their shareholders will accept lower levels of return on credit but that is just not the case. The capital equation is therefore a difficult one.

Equally, the banker sector is more consolidated and concentrated now than it was before the crisis, so the idea of more competition rather than less as a result of these issues is also incorrect.

Ronnie Chan: If the question is whether the financial systems is healed or not, I think we have not even gone to see the doctor yet. Many of the issues are not even addressed. Let's face it, the Western financial system is far better than the Asian, but it is not a perfect systems and we need to address the issues we face.

I still think that commercial banking and investment banking should not mix for example. They do not belong in the same house and yet no-one is talking about Glass-Steagall and bringing it back. We need to do that as we need to define these parameters in the banks. Unless we define between and separate these sorts of banks, we still have issues.

The Extraordinary Madness of Banks

Some people are even talking about shadow banking coming back already, and I fear that unless commercial and investment banking are put into a clearer perspective we will have all these issues again.

There's a problem with regulation as well, both under- and over-regulation depending upon where you look. By definition, regulation will always be behind product design and that is something we need to address, as many do not know of risks until after they occur.

On the final area, about the argument that we have to pay good bonuses to get the best brains, I would argue that if, by eliminating bonuses we lose those brains, then hallelujah.

Bill White: There's a question about a return to normalcy and getting back to equilibrium, but we haven't talked about rolling back all that leverage yet, all those CDOs, ABSs, MBOs, SIVs etc, so we're not out of the woods yet. We also worried about banks being too big and too complex to fail and yet now, two years into this crisis, the banks are even bigger and more complicated than ever before and every big bank is a universal bank mixing investment and commercial banking.

My concern is that these big banks will turn out to be zombie banks, and that they are too impaired to get the economic fuel moving again. Another concern is that they'll now get even more cavalier than they were before the crisis, and credit lending standards will deteriorate further as a consequence.

Mervyn King said that if a bank is too big to fail then it's not a viable bank, and that's where we need to focus for the future of regulation. In fact, I agree with Lord Turner of the FSA's view that we need every bank to create a 'living will'. Institutions must have plans to close themselves down lodged with the regulators, and if they cannot show that plan to the regulator then they must unbundle themselves from their complexity until they can, as Lord Turner has proposed.

Peter Sands: There's much here that I agree with but where I do not is if we go for any form of new Glass-Steagall lite. That is just a distraction. It wouldn't work. Supposedly we can have narrow banks that can go bust and that's alright. This would be the Bear Stearns, Washington Mutual, Northern Rock. What you actually get through Glass-Steagall in this case, however, is regulatory arbitrage which was a key contributor to the crisis. Therefore I think we need to regulate institutions regardless of what business they're in rather than trying to narrow their business.

The idea of a living will is also flawed in that, if you only rely upon regulation to restrain entrepreneurial exuberance, you will undoubtedly get another crisis. You need market discipline too. So we should be looking for who is too big to fail, what would happen if they did and a market discipline to manage that uncertainty.

I also don't like the phrase 'living will'. A will is meant to be the spreading of your assets that you distribute to your heirs whereas, for a bank, it is the opposite. How do you distribute your problems to others if you fail?

Martin Wolf: What about future growth then?

Peter Sands: Markets are thrilled that we're not disappearing over a cliff but no-one knows where we are going next. The view used to be that the world had this model where Asia produced and the West consumed but that model has gone. So where is the growth of demand going to come from? That is a structural issue and will be a reflection of domestic demand and balances across the emerging economies to rectify rather than the West, and that will take time. So there is a risk that this recovery will slow or stutter.

Bill White: We have very, very deep-seated problems here that could have led to bad deflation as in debt deflation. Well, the authorities stepping in and using Keynesian methods stopped all that. But what have been the side effects? What are the long-term

123

implications of those responses to deflation? I worry about that. In fact, I worry about three specific things.

First, inflation. This is not a long-term thing as the issues are deflationary today but with quantitative easing, deflationary issues may come unstuck at some point. We've seen this in Latin America and over many decades perceptions of changes in the monetary regime can have a big impact on the economy. It will be very hard to know how to tighten things when needed. So I worry about deflation short-term and inflation long-term.

The second thing I worry about is asset prices. Yet again we are trying to get out of things the way we did last time, by generating another asset bubble. I worry about that.

Lastly, I worry about what many of the governments are doing is getting in the way of the structural adjustments that are required to correct the economy. We have industries that are too big – the auto industry, construction industry, banking industry – along with geographical imbalances between importers and exporters. Then the UK and USA does this 'cash for clunkers' deal and I take the view that the car industry is too big and what do we do? We create false demand and incentives to buy more cars to make the industry even bigger, which got us into the issue before: an industry that is too big.

So I'm worried about everything.

Peter Sands: I think a lot of this crystallises about what happens with the dollar and we can see a very volatile future for the dollar. China has an exquisitely balanced equation between wanting to see the dollar play a less dominant role as the reserve currency, but then they also have a lot of dollars and don't want to lose the value of that investment.

Ronnie Chan: China cannot save the world as it's not big enough – China has a $4tn GDP versus $40tn amongst the largest group of seven others,

True, they pumped $200bn into the economy every month for several months, but what sectors are they stimulating? Infrastructure, and that is government-led. That is the sector doing its job.

You are not dealing with an economy that is purely market driven either, but one that is still centrally led. So they can drive change.

You don't change 3,000 years of frugality being a virtue as a culture in a few months.

Peter Sands: I think there have been some positive developments in regulation in terms of the Financial Stability Board, the dialogue globally, the acceptance of a need to be coordinated and consistent in reponse. This is a significant step forward. As an industry we do need better regulation as good banks get damaged by bad regulations.

There is a danger that we maybe get too focused upon this particular crisis and the closing of the stable doors for just these issues, which creates another set of issues downstream. I think we are doing this in some ways.

Equally, we are potentially creating an industry of overly complex and opaque regulation, by having too many cooks spoil the broth in terms of risk managers, compliance officers, accountants and auditors all in there trying to add to the equation. We also maybe get too embroiled in all the risks of liquidity and credit, and lose sight of what it is we are here to do as banks. There were issues in this area in Basel II for example, and there is a danger of more of this happening now.

There's too much focus upon the institutional structures of regulation as well, such as the UK's debate about who has control: the FSA, the Bank of England or the Treasury. The debate should be more about what regulators can do and should do well. Many of the failures of regulation were not because they couldn't do something but because they failed to execute their duties properly. That is not to excuse the bankers, but if we don't have the right rules, well executed and to work against, then we don't have a clear path forward.

Bill White: There's a lot of people focusing upon what was new that went wrong and say that if we could just fix all of that then all will be good. There is one camp, for example, who just want to tackle SIVs and CDOs and just fix that. But we should focus upon what was the same that caused this and other crises. The underlying issues that led to previous collapses. We are going to address these by taking the systemic issues and placing them front and centre this time.

So, bank CEO, tell me what you think ... (2009)

The Banker magazine hit the mark again this month with a research report on CEOs' views. During February and March, they surveyed 87 bank CEOs across Western (6.5%) and Eastern (15.6%) Europe, North (5.2%) and South (14.3%) America, Africa (20.8%) and Asia (23.4%).

The figures in brackets are the percentage of CEOs from each region responding, and here's a summary of key results.

Will business be better or worse in 2009 compared to 2008?

28.7% expect business to be better;
31% expect business to be a little worse; and
11.5% expect business to be a lot worse.

Comment: if one CEO was Canadian, then Western European and the USA would equal around 11.5%, about the same number that expect things to be a 'lot worse'!

When will we recover?

Q2 2009	25.3%,
Q3	9.2%
Q4	23.0%
1H 2010	17.2%
2H 2010	19.5%
2011+	5.7%

That means approximately 57.5% of CEOs expect recovery this year ... interesting that South America, Africa and Asian CEOs equal 57.7% of respondents, which means American and European CEOs may be looking to next year.

What were the main causes of the crisis?

1. Exotic financial structures
2. Excessive leverage
3. Global macroeconomic imbalances creating excessive liquidity
4. Poor regulation
5. Poor management

48.2% described their capital levels as higher than regulatory requirements, whist only 3.5% thought theirs was too low (Citi? BoA? RBS?).

50.6% expect their balance sheet structure to stay the same, whilst 15% thought a significant restructuring would be needed ... woohoo!

A key question for those in my community was:

Where do you see investment areas in 2009?

71.3%	IT systems
64.4%	Core banking systems
63.2%	The bank's retail network
56.3%	Compliance

The Extraordinary Madness of Banks

36.8%   Customers surveys
29.9%   New staff
25.3%   Environmentally friendly technology
24.1%   CSR projects

In other words, bugger the planet … we're more interested in survival and prosperity!

Some other interesting notes include:

◆   40% of CEOs reported retail savings and deposits are the most active business are for the bank and 25.3% said that corporate lending is the most active area; less than 5% said that mortgage lending would be the most active area; and

◆   Asked how governments can help banks, less than a third answered through quantitative easing … is that why the Treasury is having second thoughts about more quantitative easing.

Financial crisis survey surprise result (2009)

I just completed a brief online survey about the financial crisis.

The question was: "What do you believe to be the most challenging factor facing (the financial) industry over the next five years?"

Here's the current result:

30% … winning back the public trust, after losing billions in people's savings;

27% … staying ahead in the technology curve to innovate and improve efficiency and customer experience;

20% … changing the personal image of the 'financial services executive' to that of a server of the greater good rather than only self-fulfilment;

14% ... working closely with the government to ensure regulations are stringent, fair and obeyed;

9% ... advocating investment and financial attention to world issues (global warming, third-world country development, infrastructure, etc.).

I've no idea how many people voted, but I do know that it's more than a few hundred and many of them are senior guys in banking.

What amazed me about this result is that 'winning back the public trust' will take years, probably decades. For example, a recent paper by the economist J K Galbraith includes this key paragraph about the recovery after the Great Depression of the 1930s:

> "What did not recover, under Roosevelt, was the private banking system. Borrowing and lending – mortgages and home construction – contributed far less to the growth of output in the 1930s and 40s than they had in the 1920s or would come to do after the war. If they had savings at all, people stayed in Treasuries, and despite huge deficits interest rates for federal debt remained near zero. The liquidity trap wasn't overcome until the war ended. It was the war, and only the war, that restored (or, more accurately, created for the first time) the financial wealth of the American middle class."

If this is the case, then investing in gaining trust will fall on stony ground for quite a while to come.

Then the second key vote, 'staying ahead in the technology curve', is also interesting.

Now I advocate that banks must be on the leading edge of technology as it is a bits and bytes business, but I don't see many banks investing in staying ahead of the technology curve right now ... and even fewer investing in staying ahead of the curve by using technology to gain back customer trust.

The Extraordinary Madness of Banks

If they were, I would be pointing out lots of examples of banks using social media to gain trust ... and yet, in the UK in particular, I find it hard to spot even one. Now there is some good news in that First Direct launched its new media news centre service last week, a first for British banks. But there are not that many banks using technology to move ahead of the curve whilst gaining trust.

The only banks doing this appear to be the one's launching customer engagement platforms using social media, such as HSBC's small business community service, First Direct's social media newsroom, Caja Navarro's social lending platform, BBVA's *Tu Cuentas*, Wells Fargo, and Bank of America.

For the banks not doing this stuff, well, they are stuffed, aren't they?

Chapter 5 **Too big to fail?**

Introduction

One of the major refrains of the Global Financial Crisis, or GFC as some refer to it, has been the discussion of whether banks can be too big to fail, or TBTF, as others refer to it. The too big to fail debate has been particularly apropos, as the whole financial crisis has been predicated upon the issues of a global interconnectivity between a very small number of banks. These banks and their worldwide influence has led to politicians and regulators considering whether to limit a bank's scale in the future and potentially to break up the banks that are over-sized today. The danger of such action is that it could potentially damage already weakened economies, as well as dramatically altering the ability for banks to compete in the future. This dilemma is one that cannot be resolved easily, with the most common suggestion being that banks can operate globally at major size and scale, but they must do so with a 'living will' that details how they would untangle the web they have woven should they ever be in a position of failure. This is not ideal, but at least some sort of compromise is better than nothing.

Let bad banks fail (2009)

I was invited to Ireland this week to join a debate at the University College Cork's Philosophical Debating Society. The debate was entitled 'This House believes that we should let banks go to the wall' – as in, banks should die if they are failing.

I offered to take either side of the debate, as I can argue my way out of a paper bag, and they gave me the proposing motion. My rival was Ciaran Hancock, Business Affairs Correspondent with the Irish and UK Times, who opposed the motion.

I don't have time to report the whole debate so I'm just going to present my one-sided view. Please bear in mind that I could quite easily have argued either corner, so these views are not necessarily my own.

Ladies and gentlemen:

The problem with our world today is that the banks have overleveraged and the implosion of credit they created is now our monster to tame. For each euro a bank owned, they generated 10 or even 100 euros of debt. That debt mountain has to be eroded before the good times can roll again.

The real question therefore, is should that debt mountain be vanquished today or in years to come?

If your answer is for years to come, then support the government's actions and pump cash into the ailing system of finance. Give this debt mountain to the next generation, as in your kids.

On the other hand, if your answer is that we should swallow our medicine now in order to get over this headache, then we should allow the banks to go to the wall. At least we can then move on with a clean sheet for the future.

I vote for the latter choice because it will make us fitter for the future, rather than having a long-term pain in the rear.

All of this started back in 2002. Back then, the leverage of credit was nowhere near as horrendous as it is today. Since then, in the five years that followed, derivatives markets created around $20 trillion of false credit – money that did not exist. This was being generated in the USA and across Europe through credit derivatives, and it created a housing bubble and world of money that was non-sustainable, non-believable and non-existent.

The fall of Lehman Brothers in 2008 ended that rollercoaster ride forever, and the consequent hard landing means that we now have to pay back that $20 trillion-plus of credit.

That is the size of this correction, in fact it could be even greater, and this is why banks should be allowed to go to the wall.

Banks should be allowed to go to the wall because the defenders of free market economics supported and promoted the efficient operation of markets. They actively defended the use of credit default swaps, collateralised debt obligations and other free market tools. They claimed these were just examples of the free markets at work. They cheerfully endorsed the self-regulation of the financial markets on the basis that only the fittest survive.

So why are they not supporting, promoting, cheering, endorsing and defending free market economics today?

In a free markets world, those that have fail are supposed to do just that: fail. The banks that are not the fittest should not survive. They should be allowed to go to the wall.

Why won't we let these banks fail therefore? Because they are 'too big to fail', 'too integral to our economy' or 'too important for society'?

No. Banks are not allowed to fail because politicians would lose their jobs and, as a consequence, our societies might run to anarchy.

If we were all allowed to lose our money on deposit and businesses were suddenly unable to process payments or gain access to capital, our economies would crash, unemployment would rise and riots would ensue.

We have seen this in Greece recently, and every day there is picketing outside the parliament of Iceland to show the anger and hurt their country is feeling.

This is the reality of letting banks fail and this would be the reality here in Ireland, across Europe and most countries impacted by this crisis.

But politicians losing their offices, bankers losing their jobs and society facing levels of unemployment and disruption is exactly what we have to face up to, if we are to get over this glitch.

Let me put it another way; if we do not swallow this pain today then we are just postponing it for tomorrow. By not letting banks fail, we are placing the burden of their debt and our gluttony on our children and our children's children. There is the rub. So we should take our medicine today and be done with it, rather than living on our greed and letting our children and grandchildren pay for it.

And even if we do not let banks fail, we do not solve the problem. We just exacerbate it.

By not letting banks fail, governments are pumping tens of billions of dollars into a system that is broken. This system is not fixable, or appears not to be. After all, the US and European governments sank over a trillion dollars into the system in October and it is still broken. These governments came back with a further multi-trillion dollar package just this month, and it is still broken.

All that the government's actions have achieved is to realign the balance sheet of the banks and line the bankster's pockets. This purely demonstrates therefore that providing liquidity from government coffers does not work.

What about nationalising the banks then? Well, that does not work either.

By nationalising the banks all you achieve is inefficiency and imbalance. You cannot have a system where some banks are government-owned and some are not. So do we nationalise all of them, including the healthy banks, just because some rotten apples have poisoned the barrel? That is not fair.

Equally, by nationalising a few, that is also not fair. The ones that are nationalised become lazy and complacent, and they will continually be beaten by the ones that are not. Furthermore, by nationalising institutions where neither the institutions themselves nor the government wants to nationalise them, we create an even worse situation.

No, let bad banks fail and be done with it.

And what would happen if we did let banks go to the wall? What would be the worst scenario? Riots, anarchy, revolution, civil war?

The Extraordinary Madness of Banks

Possibly ... but only if we let all the banks fail, including the good ones. Equally, there are alternatives.

For example Joseph Stiglitz, the Nobel Prize winning economist, believes that banks should be allowed to fail. The way he would do it is to have the government guarantee and secure all depositors' monies, along with the current bank operations, buildings and branches. The government then wipes out their balance sheet debts by declaring the banks bankrupt and, through the same process, they then create new banks that are healthy. When the new banks prove to be robust, they are then returned to the private sector with a clean bill of health.

This approach has some merit, as it focuses upon creating good banks. After all, who wants to create 'bad banks'? Who wants a 'toxic bank'? What is the point of that?

Let the bad banks fail.

And let us not forget that we are not saying let all banks fail. Just the ones that are broken. There are still healthy banks out there and, in the rules of free market economics, these banks should be allowed to be more powerful and competitive at the expense of the ones that are ailing and weak. Let the fittest survive and let the weakest go to the wall.

Equally, in a world where technology is a critical component, there are many new ways of gaining access to finance anyway, with several new financial providers in play.

In the UK, we have seen several new banks being launched by local governments, the Post Office, Metro Bank and more. We have also seen new providers such as Zopa, Wonga, SmartyPig and the Barter Network, to name but a few.

There are healthy banks and alternative banks therefore who can prop up our system.

Result? If the ailing and weak banks that over-leveraged cannot cover their capital, then let them fail. Others will be left standing that are efficient and appropriate. This is how free market economics works, and I wonder why the free market economists and politicians don't get this.

In conclusion, the real reason we won't let bad banks fail is because politicians are too fearful of losing their jobs and society is too concerned about losing the good times.

But here is the core of the reason banks should be allowed to go to the wall: if we don't lose jobs and the good times now, then someone will lose them later. And that someone is you, your children and your children's children.

All we are doing is deferring the issue through stimulus packages to saddle future generations with debts and taxes. Equally, as George Osborne the UK's Shadow Chancellor, recently stated, we have allowed the capitalisation of the profits through the socialisation of the losses. Banksters enjoyed the freedom of the city in the good times whilst giving us all the hurt for the bad times.

This is wrong.

So let the systems fail, the bad banks go to the wall, the cleansing of the system and its cancerous over-leveraged poison, and create a new world order that works far better than the broken one of today.

Thank you.

My opponent then presented some thoughts about how government guarantees meant that we were not deferring taxes to future generations; how 30,000 bankers on the dole queues would not be right; that AIB and other banks had announced lending was coming back to SMEs and more; that the government could not do the job the banks do; that 100,000 people would be laid off in Ireland this year with unemployment rising to 12% of the population; that growth was down 6% this year and was only getting worse; and so on.

His bottom line was that we could not let the banks go to the wall, as all of this would just get worse and that was untenable.

We then had a long debate with the audience of students and Corkonians (no, people from Cork are not called Corkers) with comments such as the fact that Anglo-Irish Bank is a disgrace which fuelled and protected property developers and no-one else; that the government's guarantees have purely underwritten foreign business loans; that the world today is characterised by insecurity and doubt and that we need security and certainty for an economy to work; that banks fulfil a role the state does not and cannot, after all where else do business start-ups have to go other than a bank for capital; that if banks fail, we fail as a society and that our property becomes their property and we all go to the wall; and more.

Finally, we came to conclusions.

I've already outlined most of what was said but, in my concluding remarks, I did say that the issue we face today is the deleveraging of our over-leverage.

When Lehman Brothers collapsed, over $550 billion was withdrawn from the US banking system in hours. This would have led to the collapse of America within a day if action had not been taken. That incident created the fear, uncertainty and doubt (FUD) we face today, and that if we do not let more bad banks fail, we can never get back to certainty and security.

The fact that every $1 billion in losses at Lehman could equate to $20 billion or more of losses on credit default swaps created the FUD. No-one knew where or with whom these losses would occur and, with $400 billion of losses, that meant the world expected up to $10 trillion of exposure.

That was, and is, the issue.

This has resulted in the strangulation of credit and access to capital, which is why Ireland is now paying €3.50 for every €100 to insure its sovereign debt, compared with only €0.10 for every €100 just a year ago.

This is unsustainable when you have public sector debt in Ireland expected to rise by €15 billion this year alone, to €70 billion overall, and 220% of the country's annual economic output pledged to the banking system.

That is why bad banks should go to the wall. There will still be good banks, there will still be new banks, but bad banks need to go to the wall.

We then had a vote and the motion was carried ... by about one vote. Banks should be allowed to go to the wall. Even with all of this emotion and reasoned argument, students and Corkonians were still split about whether banks should be allowed to fail.

But then, with lots of money in savings for the pensioners in the room and a debating society full of budding lawyers (yes, that's the core group of graduates in a debating room), it's not surprising the motion was only just carried. After all, who wants to see a bank fail when they are either providing your current or future income?

We believe banks should (not) fail? (2009)

In response to the question 'Why should banks be allowed to fail?' a friend of mine gave me three sheets of neatly written paper arguing the case. As this came from a banker, it had me worried.

So, here are 20 reasons to let banks go under:

1) To protect sovereign indebtedness – can governments truly afford to prop up the banking systems with their promises?
2) It's better to jail bankers than politicians, so let them fail and hang the bankers responsible.
3) By letting banks fail, at least you can apportion blame and punish those responsible.

4) Let the banks fail that should fail, and the markets will return to normality sooner rather than later

5) Let the banks fail, as the taxpayer will not be held responsible at least.

6) The industry has to restructure anyway so, by letting the banks fail, this can happen sooner rather than later.

7) If banking is meant to be free trade with principles based regulation, then this can draw a line to say that model is broken. The banks don't work and the state should not take a strong arm in systems that are meant to be 'free'.

8) If the USA can let Lehman fail, why should we prop up our ailing banks?

9) Let banks fail because it will accelerate reform in the industry.

10) Bonuses, compensation culture, infectious greed ... let banks fail as it will define the limits of moral hazard in these markets.

11) Let banks fail as it will allow investors to pick up the best parts of banks that were working whilst letting the bad parts rot with government.

12) Let banks fail ... who would vote for a national 'bad bank' to be created at the taxpayers' expense?

13) We need a national review of bank culture, rewards and practices and this would allow one to take place.

14) By letting banks fail, the government guarantees could be revoked and the size of the issue made known.

15) The market needs new models for lending and this would allow the markets to create them.

16) It would get rid of this idea that banks can do what they want and the state will protect them.

17) Let our banks fail as it will allow the state to adopt international standards and best practices.

18) If you let the banks fail, the government cannot be charge with cronyism (giving jobs to their banking friends).

19) Let the banks fail and the government undermines any opposition form other parties as they can show they did the 'right thing'.
20) Let banks fail as the system is so corrupt that it would create a new world order and, hopefully, a better one.

Well, there are 20 good reasons to let banks fail, and they all came from a banker!

The pros and cons of bank nationalisation (2009)

For the past year, we have watched financial institutions regularly being nationalised, part nationalised or effectively nationalised in all but name. We happily accept that this is right, as banks are 'too big to fail'.

But is it right? Is nationalisation a good or a bad thing?

Most folks who grew up under Margaret Thatcher, Ronald Reagan and the Cold War years, think that nationalisation is a swear word. They were ingrained in privatisation bids and offers, the de-nationalisation of everything that was nationalised, and the belief that free markets reign supreme. Milton Friedman was the one and only economics voice worth listening to, and businesses should be allowed to fail if they cannot compete.

The result?

AT&T was broken up, British Airways had to fly free and all public institutions were scrutinised in exact detail to see if they were really in the public interest. Public-Private Partnerships flourished, and lots of folks made a lot of money from privatisations.

Two decades later, we all wonder whether this was right.

On reflection, maybe not. We now look at 1929 and think that John Maynard Keynes was the right one, and that we should allow the word nationalisation back into our lingo.

The Extraordinary Madness of Banks

So, in the context of financial services, is nationalisation a good or a bad thing?

In the past week alone, we have seen the nationalisation of Anglo-Irish Bank and the nationalisation in all but name of the Royal Bank of Scotland. Germany's effectively nationalised HypoReal Estate, whilst the USA has all but nationalised Citibank, Fannie Mae, Freddie Mac, AIG and the rest.

Nationalisation isn't so bad after all ... but I can see a few reasons for and against such tactics so let's debate it for a minute.

Unusually, let me start with the case against nationalisation.

First, nationalised institutions are lazy and rubbish. They have no customer interest at heart, are a complete monopoly with no competition, and politicians and civil servants have no idea how to run a business. The result is that you just get big, fat, incompetent, useless operations, managed abysmally. They are happy to run like this because they lift their money directly from taxpayers' pockets and therefore have no worries about funding.

Second, nationalised institutions do nothing to move things forward. They just keep their engines running with incremental spending. The result is that there is zero innovation or creative thinking. Nationalised institutions aren't there to innovate, they're just there to operate.

Third, if nationalisation is such a good thing, then why did we tell China to stop it? In the case of China, the state-owned banks were accused for years of serving the state's interests and not the people's. China's citizens were encouraged to save and not borrow, they pooled all their monies into the state's banks which treated them like victims rather than customers, and the state moved all that money into state projects, such as railroads, farming and manufacturing.

Then, in 2001, China was told to open up the banks to competition and free market forces if they wanted to join the World Trade Agreement and start trading freely with the world. Result:

China has been opening up its banking market and allowing foreigners to compete and invest. They have move from nationalised banks to privatise banks because the world's market dictate that this is the way it has to be.

It's obvious: banks owned by governments are a bad thing.

So that's the argument against nationalising banks. Let's look at the arguments for nationalisation. The banks are buggered, business is being strangled by a lack of funding, the economy is trashed, and politicians are about to be voted out of office due to the wholesale funding markets becoming drier than a desert in the summer.

Motion carried. Let's nationalise the banks.

Why the UK government cannot nationalise (2009)

I wrote the last piece about nationalisation, because I was reflecting upon the challenges involved in the banking sector right now. The bottom line is that shareholder confidence has disappeared in the sector, especially in the UK.

For example, on 12th December I put a chart together for one article as follows:

	Share price 52 week		12/12 2008	Loss of value	Market cap* (£bn)	Market cap high (£bn)	Shareholder losses (£bn)
	High	Low					
HBOS	836.00	56.50	70.0	91.6%	£3.83	£45.74	£41.91
RBS	495.25	40.20	55.5	88.8%	£21.94	£195.78	£173.84
Barclays	576.00	117.20	143.7	75.1%	£12.03	£48.22	£36.19
Lloyds TSB	510.00	115.00	131.5	74.2%	£7.96	£30.87	£22.91
HSBC	938.00	605.25	700.5	25.3%	£84.86	£113.63	£28.77

* as at 14:00 on 12 December 2008

The Extraordinary Madness of Banks

Today, these shares have bounced up a little, but they are still trading low.

But the UK government will find it nigh on impossible to nationalise these banks, anyway. First, because no-one wants them to, unless they really have to. Second, because some of these banks are so globalised, that it would not be in the UK taxpayers' interest to do so.

Take RBS. Now, I hate to kick a man when he's down, but I did have a pop at Sir Fred in a US article yesterday. Why? Because, in retrospect, the sheer arrogance of buying ABN AMRO to p**s off John Varley was just idiotic, and the price paid was stupid.

But if the government was forced to nationalise RBS, what would they do with Citizens, Charter One, ABN AMRO and all the other overseas operations and businesses? It is surely not in the UK's interest to fund overseas markets and operations, particularly if the UK taxpayers would lose billions by doing so.

Nope. If the UK government did nationalise RBS, it would just have to sell off all those overseas businesses, losing us billions more in the process.

That's one reason why RBS has to stay private. Another blockage, however, is that, in this globalised world, some banks just cannot be invested in because they are owned by overseas organisations. For example, Barclays Bank turns out to have a clause from its last investors, the Abu Dhabi royal family, that makes it impossible for the government to get a stake in the bank.

These global movements make national governments powerless. So what is the solution?

Well, I've mentioned it many times, but a shareholder guarantee scheme has to be the way as we need shareholder confidence to get the banks back on track and Tier 1 capital to raise.

Howsabout a guarantee for retail investors only, not hedge funds or others, that if they buy bank shares today and hold them for five years, the government guarantees they will make up the difference for any losses on those shares, should there be any.

At least that would mean that the money to prop up our banks was coming from commercial market forces rather than taxpayers' pockets.

Chapter 6 The bonus issue

The
**Complete
Banker**

Introduction

Every day, the press has been attacking 'greedy' bankers over bonuses and pay. This is because the banks, particularly the investment banks, pay excessive amounts to their star performers. Policymakers have tied to deal with these issues by taxing bonuses at the highest levels possible and considering placing limits on the amounts that are paid. None of these policies really work, however, as banks are experts in both avoiding taxes where possible and, if not possible, moving locations and offices to places where the tax burden is minimal. For example, when London increased taxes to 50 percent for people earning over £150,000 – which would therefore cover most investment bankers – many moved to Geneva and Hong Kong where tax rates are considerably lower. This also means that the UK government loses important income, as a banker based in Geneva or Hong Kong takes all of their earning and those of their gardeners, housekeepers, mistresses and mates with them. Therefore, the bonus issue will continue to be a media football, a policymaker's headache and a banker's focus.

Survival of the richest (2010)

It's been a difficult time for City bankers, what with all the flak over bonuses and easy money after almost bankrupting the world.

The longest lasting row relates to bonuses and remunerations packages. This hit the headlines a year ago, and the argument still rumbles away. Put 'bank bonuses' into Google, for example, and over 10 MILLION results are returned.

That's 10,000,000. That's almost a quarterly bonus for an investment bank's senior executive and obviously is something that causes a lot of emotion.

Most of the emotion is the resentment that someone is getting paid squillions for doing diddly-squat. After all, it has been shown on many occasion that a monkey could get as good a result as most stockpickers, but that's not the point. The point is that the City traders who return the most profit to the bank get paid the most. And everyone who is part of a team that returns any profit will get something.

Just a million maybe. But something. And if you don't pay it, then the team leaves, lock, stock and two smoking cigars.

This culture is so ingrained that there are books about it, with my favourite being David Charters: 'At Bonus Time, No-One Can Hear You Scream'. It's a short book about "one man's quest for his annual bonus – in a world where ambition, terror, insecurity and desperate deeds are as natural as organic bread."

Yep, that describes it pretty well. The City is a cut-throat, testosterone-driven world.

But let's just look specifically at the UK issue. The banks are paying bonuses that seem excessive. The government is unpopular it is blamed for the bankers' excesses.

The government wants to therefore clamp down on any excess bonus payments.

But it can't. There's the rub. The UK cannot clamp down on bank bonuses, even with Alistair Darling's damp squib of a bonus tax, because one country cannot act on its own on this issue. Not unless they want to lose their banking industry and see it all go overseas.

Apparently no-one believes that will happen, although Boris Johnson thinks it will. Boris, the Mayor of London, claims that 9,000 bankers are likely to move out of London if there is a punitive singular UK tax regime in this space.

Equally, the *Financial Times* has discovered that many City banks and bankers are thinking about upping sticks:

"A couple of years ago colleagues of mine would say to me how much they loved London, what a great place it was to live," says a US-born banker at a European investment bank. "Now they're tired of being here. They feel under attack.

"Trading is the most mobile investment bank business that could be shifted abroad. And while many banks have show-off, state-of-the-art trading floors in London – such as Bank of America Merrill Lynch's at their European headquarters behind Saint Paul's Cathedral – few would have any compunction about pragmatically shifting a portion of staff to more attractive financial centres.

"A quarter of staff could be easily relocated," says one European investment bank boss. He estimates that within six months, 5,000 to 10,000 City bankers could be shifted to another European centre such as Frankfurt or Zurich."

So what does this mean in reality? The reality is that the UK cannot unilaterally restrict bank bonuses without losing significant tax and income across the UK.

First, if 9,000 bankers leave then that is 9,000 x (salary + bonus). In reality therefore, if each banker earns an average of £2 million or so all up, it's a loss of about £20 billion to the UK economy and taxation of around £5 billion or more. That's a serious amount of income to the Treasury and commerce across Britain, and London in particular, that disappears up the spout. No wonder the *Evening Standard*'s recent poll of Londoners found that 68% of readers feel that bumper City bonuses are good for London's economy.

But it's more fundamental than this. If 9,000 bankers leave London, then it is also 9,000 x 4 jobs. Each banker supports an infrastructure across London of accountants, lawyers, cleaning staff, receptionists, security guards, catering, bars, restaurants and more. All of the support and infrastructure that services their offices and complex negotiations, in other words. So it's more like 36,000 job losses rather than 9,000.

OK, the other 27,000 aren't necessarily earning £2 million a year, but let's say they average £20,000 per year, the UK's average median salary (not London, UK).

This would mean a loss of a further £540 million in income, £100 million-plus in taxation and a further 27,000 or more on the unemployed and social security benefit numbers.

Following on from this, wherever the bankers move to will also become a major financial centre and hence other firms might follow, paving the way for a mass exodus, in worst-case scenario.

In best-case scenario, it would just mean that London loses its shine as a financial centre, which is threatened already. For example, HSBC has made moves for its CEO to relocate to Hong Kong and is listing on the Shanghai Exchange over the past few months, and many report that Shanghai will outshine London by 2019.

So all in all, the Treasury and Gordon Brown have a big challenge, and it's not a simple one, of cracking down on bonuses with a stupid media-pleasing bonus tax that, in reality, means nothing (the banks just changed 'bonus' to 'salary', and gave everyone a temporary three-month £1m pay rise).

No, this needs co-ordinated global action which is why London is working very closely with Brussels, Washington and other economic centres to try to create a joint agreement on this thorny issue. Without a joint agreement, one by the whole G20 (not just France and the UK), any action taken in London to limit bankers' bonuses will be detrimental to the Treasury, the economy and the country as a whole.

The UK banking sector contributes significantly to the UK and its economy:

◆ Employing almost half a million people with the wider financial industry employing over 1.1 million;
◆ Together with related activities (accountancy, business, computer and legal services, etc), some three million people rely on the financial industry for their jobs;

151

- Banks and financial services contribute £70 billion to the UK's national output (6.8% of GDP);
- Banks and financial services provide 25% of total corporation tax (£8 billion) to the UK government;
- The value of foreign exchange business passed through London every day is £560bn ($1 trillion).

Ending the never-ending bonus war (2010)

I'm fed up with the argument about bonuses and cannot believe it still rumbles on after a year of debate and G20 meetings. With Barclays announcing record profits last week, and therefore increased bonuses, the media latched onto this angle more than the fact that Barclays, UBS, Goldman Sachs and others demonstrates reviving markets and a recovered financial sector.

Sure, bonuses are irritating ... but only because we don't get them, the guys who do are as reliable as stockpickers as monkeys, and no-one knows how to break out of this cycle of paying millions for a job that is demanding, but no more so than many.

So here's my suggestion as to how it could be resolved.

First, set a regulatory limit on the bonus pool and the size of an individual's bonus payment.

For example, limit the bonus pool allocation to no more than 33% of the bank's full year profit after tax across all bank subsidiaries, as shareholders and capital reserves must have an equal recognition. This means that profit should be apportioned equally – one third – to each constituency. Then limit individual bonus payments to a cap of 0.1% of full year profits after tax.

For example, Barclays net profit was £9.39 billion in 2009, up from £4.38 billion a year earlier. £9.39 billion profits would create a maximum bonus to any one trader of £9.39 million. That may seem a lot, but it's been a good year and is far less than some of the current payouts. Equally, if you take Barclays profits from the year before, it would have been £4.38 million. A mere pittance compared to today's bonus culture but, if you have a level playing field, far better than today's excesses. And this is looking at a decent bank result.

Meanwhile, take a bank like Royal Bank of Scotland (RBS). The rules above would be extremely punitive for them. It doesn't necessarily outlaw any bonuses within RBS, but it does challenge the bank as to how to create a bonus pool when there is no profit.

But look at the wording. It says the bonus pool 'cannot exceed' a third of group profits, not that it must be a third. Therefore, for RBS, they can allocate bonuses. In fact, they have to in order to retain talent and remain competitive.

Nevertheless, you would want to ensure that a loss-making bank allocated bonuses that were in the best interests of the bank. As a result, the stipulation should be that the bonus plan and allocations for all banks are approved by an independent panel comprising a cross-section of the shareholders of the bank. Approval of the plan must be agreed by a majority – greater than 66 percent – of the panel, and the panel must comprise a minimum of ten investors including at least three retail investors.

The selection and choice of panel members must be approved by the home regulator and, whatever the panel size, a minimum of one-third must be retail shareholders rather than institutional. This should ensure a bonus pool and payout that seems agreeable to all shareholders, and therefore should also keep the regulator and media quiet.

All of the above may sound reasonable (or not), but then you have the other key question which is: how would you ensure these caps are adhered to?

After all, any government who contemplated the above would just find all of their banks moving to the Cayman Islands or Switzerland to avoid such punitive arrangements.

The Extraordinary Madness of Banks

OK, so let's stop that one at the same time by declaring that, for a bank to operate in certain markets – especially the G20 nations – the bank must be registered in a country that has signed up to and been recognised as implementing the G20's taxation agreement.

This taxation agreement is based upon banks regulated under the new Tobin tax regime (oh yes, if you didn't think it was going to happen, it will!). From the *FT*:

> "For years, taxes on capital flows were seen as a barbarous relic of the 70s, on a par with Demis Roussos and Baked Alaska. No friend of free markets dared support the idea of US economist James Tobin, dreamed up to curb currency volatility after Bretton Woods collapsed. That's changing. Since Lord Turner, chairman of the UK's Financial Services Authority, started stirring interest in taxing financial transactions last year, politicians in Germany, France and Australia have voiced tentative approval. Now Japan, through the musings of vice-finance minister Naoki Minezaki, might just be falling in line."

So, the first thing is that the bank must be headquartered and file accounts in a recognised G20 Tobin tax location.

Second, the banks' accounts must be filed in that country and show a detailed breakdown of profits and losses using IFRS accounting, not GAAP (ouch, that might hurt).

Third, and most crucially, the bank must declare any movement of funds or debt to a location that falls outside the G20 Tobin tax coverage, such as the Cayman Islands or Costa Rica. This is to ensure that complex debt equity swaps, such as the Barclays transaction that took place last September, are registered, regulated and monitored to ensure that this is legitimate tax avoidance and not evasion.

All of the above would ensure that banks and their individuals on major bonus deals, could not just up sticks and move to a location outside the grip of the bonus rules as, if they did, they would effectively be removing themselves from the markets where they need to trade – the G20 markets.

Anyways, it may not solve or cover all the ground required – as I'm no lawyer or accountant – but at least this would be a start.

I think what's bugging everyone right now is that this crisis began in August 2007 – almost two and a half years ago – and blew up into a full blown meltdown almost 18 months ago in September 2008. So here we are, years after this all began, with bailed-out banks, angry taxpayers, a full-blown recession and all the news is of investment markets behaviours remaining unchanged.

That's what's bugging everyone ... so come on G20, pull yer finger out, get some actions started, and put an end to this never-ending bonus debate.

Bankers deserve their bonuses (2009)

I know that this will cause an argument, as I was having this very argument myself, but I cannot let the opportunity pass to report a conversation I was having about City bonuses.

The media have a blast every time there's a rumour of a bonus being paid in a bank, but here's the rub: bankers deserve their bonuses.

Put it in context. You go out for a meal and have great service – do you purposefully not tip the waiter or waitress, just because you happen to know that the restaurant is making losses?

You are a branch teller. You sit there every day smiling and chatting with customers, counting money, behaving honestly and doing a good job. Do you not deserve to be paid for meeting objectives, as per your job contract, even though the bank is losing money?

You're working in a bank call centre. You work really hard every day, taking abuse over the phone. You achieve all of your targets and receive the Best Call Centre Worker of the Year Award. Do you not deserve the holiday in the Canary Islands that comes with the award?

You see, what gets me, taking the examples above, is that everyone in society from the highest to the lowest, from the meekest to the mildest, from the most arrogant to the most humble, would probably agree that, given the way you are employed and rewarded, you deserve your rewards.

If you agree that you would be a Scrooge if you go to a restaurant and hotel and don't tip for good service, then surely you agree that if you employ a branch or call centre worker, and don't pay them for achieving their annual objectives, you are behaving badly too.

If you were working in an IT firm, retail store or similar operation, would you not pay staff bonuses to call centre and store workers, even if the firm as a whole made a loss? You probably would if you could.

So now we get on to the fact that we are talking about banks. Just because the bank's management and investment managers screwed up, does it really mean that every worker in a branch or call centre should be punished? Shouldn't staff be rewarded if they achieved their targets and worked honestly and hard, with dedication and conscientiousness?

So now you may be getting a little convinced that yes, some of these folks deserve their £2,000 annual reward for good service or holiday in the Canary Islands ... if you're not convinced, then why not? Surely it is the bank's management that should be punished, not the dedicated staff who worked hard for them and had no idea what a SIV, CDO, MBA, CDS and the rest was all about.

So now to the really contentious part. If a waiter in a restaurant deserves their tip, even if the restaurant is losing money; if

156

the housekeeper in the hotel deserves the few pounds that you left for them, even though the hotel is losing money; then the call centre worker and branch teller deserve theirs. If you would reward the call centre worker in a retail business, even when the retailer is making losses, then you should reward the bank call centre worker.

So what's the difference between that, and the investment banker who made the bank £10 billion profit last year? Why should the investment banker lose his bonus of £20 million, when he achieved all of his objectives, worked hard and in a dedicated fashion?

Oh yes, because the bank is losing billions and is being bailed out by the government. Because the investment bankers are all greedy bastards, and should be flagellated in public.

Well, I'm sorry, none of that makes sense, because didn't you just agree that the call centre worker deserved their reward for achieving objectives? What's the difference between the call centre worker and the investment banker? They both worked hard and in a dedicated fashion; they both achieved their objectives; they both had an expectation that was met and even exceeded; so why are you being so mean and saying they don't deserve it?

Oh yes, because the investment banker is being paid £20 million whilst the call centre worker is being paid £2,000. So it's just a matter of scale is it?

That doesn't work then. Do you think the £2 tip versus the £2,000 reward for meeting objectives versus the £20 million bonus for producing profits should really be changed, just because you don't like the size of the last figure?

Well, the investment banker generated £10 billion in profitability for the bank, and is getting a £20 million bonus, so that's 0.2% of profit. 0.2% of profit is the banker's bonus on the profit he or she personally delivered. The call centre worker? £2,000 for achieving objectives in the call centre role that delivers ... good

The Extraordinary Madness of Banks

service? Smiling customers? No profit or, at least, a profit you cannot measure?

So now you've been convinced to give someone a reward for delivering nothing but smiles, whilst arguing not to reward someone who delivered millions in profitability.

Just because the bank lost billions elsewhere wasn't their fault. Just because the bank's management is incompetent isn't their fault. Just because the bank had to be bailed out by the government with taxpayer's money isn't their fault. The fact is that they were employed to do a job and deliver specific result, which they delivered above and beyond expectations.

And, even in today's current hostile climate, if you feel a waiter or housekeeper deserves their tip, that a call centre worker in a retail business deserves their annual bonus for achieving objectives, then you also agree that a branch teller deserves their reward, as does the investment banker.

Just because the scale of these things is massively different, is no argument to deny someone their due. Just because the bank's management is incompetent, is no excuse to break someone's employment contract. And just because the taxpayer is shelling out to pay for such incompetence is no reason to go on a witch-hunt of those people who did their jobs with honesty, dedication and tenacity.

So stop whinging about bank bonuses and start focusing upon who should be made to pay.

Who's that again? Oh yes … the management.

Bankers deserve bonuses? You're an idiot! (2009)

Further to my promotion of the idea that bankers deserve their bonuses, here's the contrarian view I could have put forward.

How could you possibly agree with the idea that bankers deserve their bonuses, you schmuck? That's just darned foolish, as bankers just do not deserve their bonuses.

In fact, President Obama is ridiculous for even allowing bankers to have any payout at all, let alone $500,000-worth. If a bank is bankrupt, has had billions from the government taken from the taxpayer's pocket, then any idea of paying a banker a bonus is just mad.

Even if a bank makes money and has had no governmental support, there should be limits. For example, yesterday there was mention of an investment banker who gets a £20 million payout for making millions for the bank. Great. But where's the clause that says he has to pay that £20 million back the year after, particularly if he or she loses the bank millions. Where is it? There is no clause to get the cash back and there's the rub: bankers make silly money in the good times but, in the bad times, they just run away with it. How foolish is that?

And then you talk about breaking a job contract, but where in the employment contract does it say that when the firm is bust you still get a payout? When I worked for a firm that went into Chapter 11, where was my bonus that year? There wasn't one of course, you dolt, because the company was bankrupt. If the firm is bankrupt of course you don't get a payout, because there's no money to pay out. So why should anyone in a bank that's losing money and going bankrupt get a payout? No way, fool! If there's no profit, there's no bonus.

Equally, you make the comparison with a waiter in a restaurant or a housekeeper in a hotel, but that's pure distraction. A banker, teller or call centre worker has nothing in common with a waiter or housekeeper, because the former have a salary whilst the latter live on their tips. You cannot even relate the two together.

Similarly, you say it's just a matter of scale, but a call centre worker or teller is typically getting a few percentage points on

The Extraordinary Madness of Banks

their salary for meeting targets that include company perform-
ance, not a thousand times salary for getting lucky in having their
bets payoff.

Bottom line: bankers don't deserve bonuses. If the firm is
losing money, then there should be zero bonus and, even if it's
making money, bonuses should be limited to some salary-related
multiple, not millions for just being lucky.

That's better, and glad to get that off me chest.

A rationale on bank bonuses (2009)

Last week, I decided to post blogs for and against bank bonuses.
I was surprised at the reactions to the case in favour, which drew
more comments on a single posting than most of my blog entries.
This is obviously an emotive subject.

By posting both sides of the debate, I can actually see that both
sides have elements of right and wrong. The truth be told, however: **those banks that would be bankrupt if the government
had not provided funding from taxpayers have zero justification to pay a bonus.**

I know that bank bosses will talk about 'contractually bound',
'it's for the folks who are deserving, such as tellers', 'if we don't pay
a bonus our best investment bankers will leave and we'll never
recover', and so on and so forth.

This is a non-argument, as the bank would be bust if it were
not for government money. There is no justification for a bankrupt bank to take government/taxpayers' money, and just give
it to those who are deserving or undeserving, as they would not
have a job right now if the bank had been allowed to fail.

This is the bottom line: if the bank were not saved, it would
not exist. Therefore, for banks that have taken government bailout pounds and dollars, any bonus should be killed.

Taking this a step further, the whole bonus culture should be reviewed anyway. If all banks stopped paying massive bonus amounts, then there wouldn't be this culture. So surely now is a good time for all the banks to just say, "OK, no more bonuses".

In particular, if the banks that are doing well did this as well as the bailed out banks, and now is as good a time as ever, then there would be no mass walkout or jeopardy. It would just kill this culture and show the stupidity of paying millions to folks who had a good, or lucky, year.

The trouble is that you then have the view that the banking world is like the football world – the best players get the best money and, if you stop paying it, they walk out.

But I think the idea of a mass walkout is a bit of a fallacy. If you don't pay your investment bankers a big bonus this year, where are they going to go? Hedge funds? Half of them have gone out of business. Another bank? There aren't many mainstream investment banks around who need them right now, and certainly not at those inflated figures.

This is not a time for concerns about mass walkouts, it's a time for concerns about the future and how to get rid of this damaging culture. To put this in context, read the classic City book, 'At Bonus Time, No-one Can Hear You Scream'. Rather than quoting from the book, here's a review by investment banker blogger Financial Crookery:

> "For many investment banks, January is the month when it happens. The phone rings, the foot soldier trots down to the honcho's office, and, with a poker face worthy of Phil Ivey, hears about a dozen words and nods non-committally. A simple ceremony at the culmination of a year's warfare. The bonus process starts around October. No, strike that.....what am I thinking. Unofficially its more like July....er..no, make that April. Yup …

"In good times, the line manager's job – let's say 'Head of Derivatives Sales' for example – is a breeze. Say the right things to the mob underneath, hire aggressively, let the market do its thing and get on with your own upwards management.

"Due to the apparent ease of this management game compared to the grisly business of finding actual customers and making them want to do profitable business with you, it is no wonder foot soldiers vie to join management ranks. Of course there are never enough proper management jobs, so important-sounding but irrelevant roles are invented to accommodate the dissemblers in good years. Yet everyone knows who pulls the strings, who is the only person who counts: the guy in front of you in January."

I think this blog entry and the book puts it all in context.

So my own personal opinion is that banks that have failed should have all their bonuses scrapped, and banks that have succeeded should have their bonuses capped. We need to get rid of this culture.

And the only bonus scheme I've enjoyed hearing about this season is Credit Suisse's, where the bonus is tied to toxic assets making good. That's a great scheme as (a) it means you have to get the things that failed to work, and (b) you have to stay around until they do.

Why are we so worried about bonuses? (2009)

I got caught up in a debate about pay and remuneration in finance this week.

This is because Stephen Hester at RBS had his package hiked to £9.6 million if he delivers all of his targets – of which the main target appears to be achieving a 70 pence share price as that will make UK plc a profit of about £8 billion – whilst Citibank and others are increasing basic remuneration and lowering bonuses to keep staff.

Now I find it interesting that folks believe pay caps, bonus cuts and other changes – such as shareholders setting executive packages – is a viable, appropriate or good thing to do.

You see, there are several issues here.

First, it is not the amount of pay we give to our leaders in financial services, or any other industry, it is the measures by which we reward them.

What you measure is what you get, as they say. And what you measure and reward first, is what you get first. And what you measure first and reward the most, is what you get delivered.

This is why financial services failed – because we measured and rewarded short-term profit without balance of the long-term risks being taken to get that profit.

It is equally why we will continue to get this wrong.

For example, many of us lament the fact that quarterly results and shareholder returns drives inappropriate management behaviours, and yet that is exactly how we are incentivising and focusing Mr. Hester at RBS.

This creates the issue where management almost solely focus upon delivering short-term results, with no thought for the long term. The idea of growing new business arenas, entering new markets, spending more on R&D, developing intellectual capital and so on and so forth, goes by the by … or bye-bye, to be honest. Who wants to invest in the future when your only measure is the next quarter's profit and the share price?

Second, if bankers can earn double in the bank next door, why are they gonna stay in this crummy place? We all talk about the fact that bankers can't find homes in other banks as they're all failing right now, but that's not true. Just look at what happened to UBS, which sued Jefferies Group Inc, saying a "massive, premeditated raid" cost the Swiss bank at least 36 healthcare investment bankers including unit chief Benjamin Lorello, or BarCap, which has been on raiding missions for analysts from Citigroup and Morgan Stanley and has been hiring aggressively. It's a dog-eat-dog world, and if you can't cut it, then get out.

Third, the markets set their own value, just as other markets such as football do. It's all based upon individual talent, and you have to pay to get the best talent. We didn't hear anyone whining about Ronaldo's £80 million move to Real Madrid or his £200,000 a week demands. Because we can see he is worth it. On a football field, the guy who scores the most goals deserves the highest wage. And so isn't it true in the financial world that the guys who create the most value deserve the highest incentives and bonuses?

Finally, a healthy bank is one that is crushing unhealthy banks, as proven above. Therefore, healthy banks are only created by having healthy income from healthy investment managers who run healthy portfolios.

It's this last point which went wrong, and it relates back to where I started.

What you measure is what you get, and what you measure and reward the most is what you get first.

Stephen Hester is being measured and rewarded on share price, and so that's where he'll focus. But then I immediately said that a pure share price focus is not good as it creates short-termism, and so I could challenge whether this is the right package for him.

Equally, if your investment teams can be lifted and dropped into another firm as a complete team, then you have to work out who you want to keep and why.

If UBS wanted to keep the healthcare team, then they should have recognised that (a) they were a healthy team; (b) they were being measured and rewarded based upon value creation and risk avoidance, and (c) they would have been rewarded based upon value creation and risk avoidance better than any package held out to them by Jefferies Group or anyone else.

And there's the rub, really. To have a strong banking system, there has to be accountability and a tie between risk and reward.

Seems obvious now.

This means that the best banks will relate risk in the long term to the rewards they provide in the short term; and they will also build-in clawback terms to any bonuses paid, such that if those bonuses blow up as high profile risk and losses in the future, they get the cash back.

Meantime, the whingers who don't like the City having big bonus bankers back in town are just jealous … I suggest they go and find a talent themselves that can pay somewhere else.

Ever tried kicking a football?

Bankers are overpaid, greedy pigs (2008)

I thought this was a good title for a blog entry although this is not me talking ... rather it seems to be a campaign with a certain associate editor and chief economics commentator at the *Financial Times* named Martin Wolf.

The campaign began a while ago, with a column entitled "Why banking remains an accident waiting to happen" in November last year. Martin's column begins:

> "Why does banking generate such turmoil, with the crisis over securitised lending the latest example? Why is the industry so profitable? Why are the people it employs so well paid? The answer to these three questions is the same: banking takes high risks. But the public sector subsidises this risk-taking. It does so because banks provide a utility. What the banks give in return, however, is gung-ho speculation."

In other words, bankers take high risks, but suffer no conse-quences as they are underwritten by governments. Certainly, with the example of Northern Rock in the UK, some may say this is true.

Then Martin picks up on another FT columnist from a week ago. The article was by Raghuram Rajan, a professor of finance at the Graduate School of Business at the University of Chicago and former chief economist at the International Monetary Fund. Raghuram writes an insightful piece entitled 'Bankers' pay is deeply flawed', with an opening line that gives away its point: "Morgan Stanley announced a $9.4bn charge-off in the fourth quarter and at the same time increased its bonus pool by 18 per cent."

Finally, we get another column by Mr. Wolf on Tuesday enti-tled "Regulators should intervene in bankers' pay", and this one's a real doozy. A few choice snippets include:

> "The world has witnessed well over 100 significant banking crises over the past three decades ... no industry has a compa-rable talent for privatising gains and socialising losses ... they know that as long as they make the same mistakes together – as 'sound bankers' do – the official sector must ride to the rescue. Bankers are able to take the economy and so the voting public hostage. Governments have no choice but to respond."

This is followed by:

> "That is so for three fundamental reasons: first, these are vir-tually the only businesses able to devastate entire economies; second, in no other industry is uncertainty so pervasive; and, finally, in no other industry is it as hard for outsiders to judge the quality of decision-making, at least in the short run. This industry is, in consequence, exceptional in the extent of both regulation and subsidisation. Yet this combination can hardly

be deemed a success. The present crisis in the world's most sophisticated financial system demonstrates that."

Followed by lots of other good stuff.

So Mr. Wolf is on a personal tirade to expose the fact that bankers are overpaid, greedy pigs who feed at the trough of society and are never held accountable as, when their excesses are untangled, all the other farm animals have to pay.

It starts to sound like something out of an Orwellian Animal Farm, with the farmers being Bush, Bernanke, Brown, Barosso and all the other politicos. The governators of the world have to tax the workers to fund these capitalist pig-dogs.

Oh, I'm sorry. Am I getting a bit too worked up here. Am I in danger of biting the hand that feeds me?

Bear in mind, it is not my voice here, but that of the *Financial Times*: the journo of the bankers and for whom I sometimes provide input.

My own view is that some bankers are overpaid ... I mean, even David Beckham might balk at the idea of being paid $160 million for being the man who led his team to relegation and lost the championship, and yet Merrill Lynch's Stan O'Neal had no such qualms. But this is only in certain parts of the market. So yes, in some areas, they are not compensated on the risks they are personally taking, but on the risks they are taking with other people's money. And many banks and bankers do blindly follow each other around the markets because they cannot bother to think for themselves.

Sure, this is true. After all, a seasoned investment banker told me years ago that bankers are lemmings, rather than pigs. They follow each other in packs and fall off cliffs, only to turn and hope they can avoid the drop at the last minute. Some do and some don't, and right now there are a number of banks teetering on that cliff-drop.

The bottom line here is not that bankers are feeding at the trough of society as overpaid capitalist pig-dogs, but that they have made a fundamental error of judgement. And the fact that they do this again, and again, and again (1985, 1987, 1998, 2000, 2007) with increasing frequency is going to put them in the public eye and open to this sort of questioning.

The fact that we have another day of reckoning just means that the media is enjoying every single moment, because most of these journos earn less than one-hundredth of the remuneration that these masters of the universe enjoy.

$110 billion? Same as my bonus (2007)

The news yesterday that the ECB, Fed and Bank of England were working together to release $110 billion of funds to buck up the markets for end of year and give the banking system confidence again was great. Hopefully, this will work and we all will live happily ever after ... although the markets don't believe it.

More importantly and irreverently, $110 billion is about the same figure as the 2007 bonus pool being paid out to all the bankers in the City and Wall Street. This was a point made in yesterday's *Times* by columnist Patrick Hosking. So it got me looking at the bonuses released so far.

Bearing in mind it's early in the season, the first to announce is Lehman Brothers. Lehman is expected to make a profit this year of around $4.13 billion. That is after writing off $700 million of subprime losses, bringing the total so far across all banks to around $77 billion of mortgage-related securities losses declared to date.

Nevertheless, by avoiding massive losses and making a profit, Lehman's CEO Richard Fuld gets a $35 million bonus and five other executives received a share of $58 million, including $29 million for the bank's President Joe Gregory, and $9 million for the Vice Chairman Thomas Russo.

Similarly, Goldman Sachs is one of the few other firms having a jolly old Christmas as they also made a profit, even though they also reported major losses of $1.7 billion for the sub-prime and $1.5 billion through algorithmic explosions during the summer. Luckily, like Lehman, Goldman achieved their profit through a successful hedging strategy to offset the mortgage related losses, meaning that they came through the credit squeeze in far better shape than their competition.

Goldman CEO Lloyd Blankfein is therefore expected to be the highest paid banker this year, with a 30% increase in pay, bringing his all-up package to be worth around $70 million.

Meanwhile, the overall bonus pool for Goldman Sachs is estimated to be over $20 billion for end of year, $3.5 billion more than last year and equating to an average $600,000 for each member of staff.

No wonder it's the Joy of Sachs, with high spirits among the big swingers, with a Christmas bash where staff have made videos taking the mickey out of various executives and managers. I'd love to get hold of one of those vids, but apparently they are all approved by the HR and PR departments beforehand. This is because so many escape onto YouTube, and they wanted to avoid any damage to reputation.

For most other banks it appears to be bad news, however, with dark clouds meaning that many are giving out zero bonuses and throwing staff into the job queues.

For example, investment analysts expect profits to be wiped out for many banks, such as Morgan Stanley and Bear Stearns, and we should remember that Citi's chucked out Chuck and Merrill's made O'Neal bail out. The news from Bank of America on Wednesday that it expects disappointing fourth-quarter results and provision for losses of at least $3.3 billion is just one of many to come, through.

The *Financial Times* summarised it all pretty well:

"Weaker-than-expected investment banking activity in November has also left analysts and executives concerned. One senior Wall Street executive, who declined to be identified by name, said: 'The credit environment in November was the worst we've seen in 20 years. There will be serious hits on subprime and near-prime residential holdings and commercial mortgage-backed securities portfolios. Everyone is going to take a hit,' he added."

This is why I'm told that UBS has capped all cash bonuses to a maximum $700,000 and is laying off 1,600 investment bankers.

Chapter 7 Solutions to the crisis – a personal view

Introduction

There are many potential solutions to this crisis. Tax banks to the hilt, limit their activities, cap their pay, inhibit their flexibility, and so on and so forth. None of these ideas particularly work and, considering activities need to be globally agreed rather than just local policies, it is hard to see how any solutions will operate that are consistent and cohesive. Within the industry there are a few co-ordinated operations and actions which may make a difference. And then there are a few ideas that are just out there for consideration. Here are a few of my own.

A Global Risk Exchange – my solution to the credit crisis (2008)

I have a solution to the credit crisis. I've labelled this my solution because:

(a) it might be rubbish;

(b) I made it up;

(c) it may be completely unworkable; and

(d) it could be very unpopular.

Therefore, I want it to be known as mine. I also want it to be known as mine because:

(a) it might be spectacular;

(b) I made it up;

(c) it could be made to work; and

(d) it might be very popular.

If it's the latter, I don't want someone else saying they made it up.

To the point, we have two problems to face immediately:

1) What do we do to get out of this mess; and

2) How to ensure we never repeat this mistake again.

Let's answer the first question: what do we do to get out of this mess? Well, here's my view, which is likely to be very unpopular among the banking community.

The fact is that we need to raise funds fast. We also need to avoid those funds solely being generated by taxpayers. We also recognise that governments cannot just generate a $700 billion amount from selling US government bonds to the Chinese. After all, why should the world's largest communist state bail out the world's largest capitalist state? By the way, as I write that line, I am trying to work out which one these days is the capitalist and which one the communist?

We need another plan which avoids taxpayer's anger and equally avoids currency degradation. Answer: take it off the thieves who stole it. This is the bit that I think would be most unpopular, but I like it.

Governments should state that all bonus payments and monies paid to investment bankers that have any association with the subprime crisis have all their assets frozen and seized by the government. This will not solve the issue, but it will appease the taxpayer.

And yes, I know that most of the funds will have already been spent or been moved overseas, but investment bankers should be accountable for these losses. Therefore, the fiscal policymakers will make it clear that any citizen who made money from toxic derivatives that led to this mess either: (a) pays it back, or (b) goes to jail for a period equivalent to one year for every million dollars missing. For Stan O'Neal that could be a very long time.

So yes, that's radical, but note that I avoided any mention of capital punishment, which George W. Bush and his cohorts must be considering. Bear in mind, that George W's home state of Texas is the one that has the most death penalties per annum!

This action would generate $5 to $10 billion in returned bonuses. That's peanuts, but boy, does it feel good.

Secondly, and also unpopular here, the US government should agree the bailout plan, but with the caveat that the banking industry will need to fund the fund from a tax on profits until it is

The Extraordinary Madness of Banks

made good. This will do nothing for bank stocks, but hey, they've tanked through the floor anyway, so what do we care? At least if it brings some stability back into the system, folks will be happier.

And both actions make us culpable and accountable for our irrational exuberance. Therefore, the industry might work harder to self-regulate itself to avoid this catastrophe ever happening again.

You may say, why punish all for the actions of the few? I suspect the government would answer: because we can and you should have gotten rid of your rotten apples before we did.

Finally, I would place an action on the treasury and regulatory players to also make them culpable and accountable. After all, they played a part in this mess. My message to them: if you ever allow any activities of this nature to remain unchecked, again, then you will be held to account. Equally, if you can demonstrate risks avoided and other miscreant ventures identified, you will be rewarded.

If the regulatory authorities missed the issues, then the key players walk ... no separation agreement, no remuneration, they just walk. Oh yes, and they are named and shamed in the process, of course. I'm even tempted to say they should be personally liable for the losses they failed to avoid, but that would put anyone off applying for regulatory office, and someone's got to do it.

This may all sound far too stick and not enough carrot, far too punitive and not enough incentive, but hey, the carrots have all been eaten. The carrots are all those annual bonuses that should not have been paid. The carrots are all those regulators who made inspection checks and missed the action. The carrots are all those shareholders who took the dividends without asking where they came from.

So that's my answer to the first question: get out of this mess by bailing out the industry, but humiliating all those culpable in the process.

Now, to the second and more important question: how do we avoid repeating the mistake?

The mistake is to let complex derivatives run unchecked. SIVs, CDSs, CDOs are the same leveraged products bringing down our industry today as the toxic meltdowns of LTCM, Enron, Worldcom and Michael Milken. It's all to do with structured finance and leveraged products being sold without any understanding of the risk or repercussions.

We basically need to create a method to avoid over-leveraged risk exposures hitting the firms which trade in the markets in the future. We also need to ensure there is an effective liquidity management engine to identify and manage total liquidity movements in the markets.

So here's how I would tackle this one. I refer you to the story of Lloyd's of London, which had risks entering and leaving the markets without any tracking. Risks would leave one door and come back through another, without anyone knowing. This only came to light when global catastrophes all occurred in the same year and Lloyd's discovered the total exposure for all those risks lay within their walls. Several Lloyd's firms went bankrupt, as did their shareholders, and everyone called for blood, change and regulation.

Their solution? A data warehouse tracking system whereby everyone in the Lloyd's markets logged every risk they took on board and the counterparties involved. Each risk had a unique identifier so that every time it left and re-entered the markets, Lloyd's could see their total exposure. Soon, any over-leveraged risks could be tracked and declined, before the markets were overly weighted against the coverage, liquidity and capital available.

We need to do this in banking. For Lloyd's, it was easier as they are all in one building. For banking, it would require a concerted effort by regulators, governments, banks and insurance firms to build a Global Risk Exchange which everyone is forced to use.

The Global Risk Exchange would log every single financial instrument traded in the world, the counterparties involved, the amounts involved, the capital against those amounts to cover the risk and other base information.

Governments would underwrite the Global Risk Exchange by stating clearly that any products traded and securitised through the Exchange would be underwritten by government backing should there be any future failures in the markets. They would do this because they would be able to see a real-time global tracking system of all risks being traded worldwide through the financial markets, the capital available to cover those risks, and where risks were leaving and re-entering to create exposures.

This is critical for our future as, right now, no-one knows how much the total losses will be from this crisis. Six months ago, it was $400 billion. Last month, it was $700 billion. Today, it's $1 trillion. No-one knows what it really is. This is because the risks have been laid off globally between banks, insurance firms, corporates and other counterparties, with no total picture of the liquidity and risk exposure involved.

So my proposal is a system to track global liquidity and risk. A Global Risk Exchange. A government endorsed entity funded by the banks.

Who would operate the system? Effectively, it's a SWIFT for risk management so SWIFT or an equivalent new body could do this.

The new firm builds a global data warehousing shared service centre, funded by the banks, that allows the exchange of risk and liquidity information using standardised messages that are globally agreed, ISO-moderated and government endorsed.

Governments effectively state that as long as the risks for securitised products that you are trading are registered on the exchange and accepted, then the product can be traded. If not, the product is declined. The acceptance of the trade is based upon the total risk and liquidity exposures, and the fact that your entry has not triggered a red light for danger. The systems. of course, will do this at light-speed through low latency engines, so don't worry about the administration, folks.

This answers the question as to how we avoid this again, by building a global risk version of SWIFT for tracking total liquidity and risk exposures between all the organisations trading globally.

So that's my plan. Be tough with the instigators and publicly flagellate them. That will get the public back on side. Then create a SWIFT for risk through a Global Risk Exchange that all governments endorse and co-operate to ensure it works.

This is not simple, and I have not even touched on the other things that are in my head, such as how we get customers back on board trusting that banks are worth doing business with.

How do we get out of this derivatives mess? (2008)

Why have we seen such a massive breakdown in the system? What was the cause? Wherein is the real blame?

The root problem: Over-The-Counter (OTC) Derivatives. There have been so many issues with these products that it amazes me how easily these products have avoided the risk and regulatory radar.

It is not to say that all derivatives products should be banned, as they have helped to create growth and wealth. However, derivatives must no longer be allowed to trade unchecked. And therein lies the rub. OTC derivatives have been traded unchecked for far too long, and the market meltdown of the past month has been created by the idiotic usage of these products.

So how will we get out of this mess?

Well, I've already proposed that we need a Global Risk Exchange, and the Chicago Mercantile Exchange (CME) with

Citadel have announced they would try and do just that for OTC derivatives, as have the Intercontinental Exchange (ICE) and the Clearing Corporation.

To resolve this, the New York Fed hosted a meeting over the weekend to work out how to agree the creation of a central counterparty for CDS contracts, in a dialogue with Eurex, NYSE Euronext, CME Group/Citadel and Intercontinental Exchange (ICE)/The Clearing Corporation. Meanwhile, the G7 issued a one-page five point plan for beating this meltdown.

This may help. It may work. Jeez, I hope it does, as we need to turn around this mess before more companies, banks, states and countries go bankrupt.

But we need more than this. After all, the five-point plan is a short-term reaction, not a long-term solution.

So here's my five-point plan, and yes, it's a radical one:

1) From Tuesday 14th October, OTC derivatives are outlawed.

2) All existing OTC derivatives are guaranteed by the G7 Ministers, and will be honoured should the contracts be activated through a credit default or other risk exposure. The method of resolution will be by the banks and fund managers involved paying all funds that are due from their commitments. However, their exposures are limited to the point at which those banks and fund managers can afford, and not allowed to rise above levels where the firm would be bankrupt. Any costs and reimbursements over and above those levels will be honoured by Treasury funding.

3) On Tuesday 14th October, a new market is opened called the ER (Electronically Regulated) Derivatives market. This market operates on the basis of a Global Risk Exchange (GRE) which will immediately be managed by the CME or ICE (toss a coin) but open to formal tender by any operator, with a final choice of operator to be selected by no later than 31st March 2009.

4) All ER derivatives can only be traded if you can prove a direct 'insurable interest' in the risks being traded. In other words, as a bank or corporation, you must be the bank or corporation that is directly involved in that bond and that risk to activate a contract. It can no longer be used for speculative purposes.

5) Any banker or fund manager discovered to be creating excessive risks in these markets through their trading strategies, and that are discovered to create market instabilities of the nature of those that we have seen in September and October 2008, will be tried under a revised Global Patriot Act. If it is proven that the individual concerned took their actions by allowing greed to overcome risk, their actions will be deemed as unpatriotic, no matter what nation or nationality they represent. The minimum sentence for such activity will be five years' incarceration with a maximum sentence of death by being hung, drawn and quartered.

That last one should put us all off ever doing this again.

How do you solve the banking crisis? (2008)

Question: How do you solve the banking crisis?
Answer: No-one knows. It's interesting to ask this question because I was asked this very question on Thursday of last week. The question was poised in the context of the UK parliament debating the Banking Bill today in the House of Commons, and I had been asked to write a briefing paper for the debate.

My answer? We need a bank shareholder guarantee scheme to encourage confidence back into the system. This is a lengthy discussion that, rather than repeat here, appeared in the Parliamentary Brief today.

Here's a very brief summary:

The Extraordinary Madness of Banks

"The government's requirement that the banking system return to the lending practices of past years is flawed because it is in direct conflict with the banks' need to recapitalise. The choice is either nationalise the whole industry and continue to pump endless cash into the system, or create a bank shareholder guarantee scheme, that protects future shareholder funds invested in the UK banks. The latter is the only way to bring back shareholder confidence and allow the banks to build more tier 1 capital based upon equity reserves, rather than just cash reserves ...

"This is a classic chicken and egg situation. The government has been feeding the chicken by giving the banks cash, but now needs to nurture the egg by focusing on the banks' balance sheets and shareholder confidence. Without the latter, we can feed the chicken as much cash as we want, but it will not make our banking system solvent. And without a shareholder guarantee scheme in UK banks, we may as well nationalise the system ...

"A healthy banking system is critical for the economy to return to stability. The government needs the banks to return to their lending policies of past years in order to maintain consumer and business confidence. However, this is in direct conflict with the needs of the banks to reserve cash in order to recapitalise to cover their solvency requirements.

"Stock market confidence in UK banks is nowhere, as demonstrated by the 0.24 per cent take-up of the recent RBS rights issue. As a result, that rights issue cost the government a further £15bn and effectively nationalises another bank.

"Without a shareholder guarantee scheme in UK banks and specific actions that encourage shareholder confidence in the UK banking system, the government will continue to have

7 : Solutions to the crisis – a personal view

to fund further banks' rights issue and fund recapitalisation. That path may as well be one to full nationalisation."

All well and good. I then spot that other people have been asked this question, and come up with totally different answers.

For example, in the *Evening Standard*, Jim O'Neill, Chief Economist at Goldman Sachs says that "There is one simple way out of the mess, Gordon: a state bank". Jim contends that the government needs to have its own bank to provide lending direct to business, and circumvent current banks completely. "A reliably financed lender might just be the key to the recovery from the current malaise we all want to see," he says.

Interesting. Especially as some regional councils, such as Essex and Kent are already creating their own banks to do just this.

So, state banks are the answer? Not according to David Cameron, the leader of the Conservative Party, who has announced plans to create a £50 million fund to guarantee bank loans to businesses.

Three different answers to the same question, and there's probably three hundred more out there.

However, I personally don't believe that either of the latter plans addresses the issue of banks' Tier 1 capital requirements. Whilst banks are dependent on pure cash reserves, rather than cash and equity reserves, we have a problem and neither of the latter plans address this.

For example, the core issue for shareholders is that a £1 investment in a bank such as RBS or HBOS a year ago would be worth less than 10 pence today.

Until banks get shareholder confidence back in the system, we will not revive this system.

www.ingramcontent.com/pod-product-compliance
Lightning Source LLC
Chambersburg PA
CBHW031934190326
41519CB00007B/526